D0784166

Careers with an Arts or Humanities Degree

Over 100 job ideas to inspire you

Caroline Barker
with
Jenny Barron and Helen Evans

Student Helpbook Series

Lifetime
Publishing

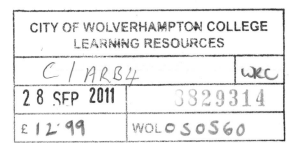

Careers with an Arts or Humanities Degree – Over 100 jobs ideas to inspire you

Fifth edition

Published by Lifetime Publishing, Mill House, Stallard Street, Trowbridge BA14 8HH

© Nord Anglia Lifetime Development South West ltd, 2010

ISBN 978-1-904979-40-1

Cover design by Arthouse Creative

Illustrations by Royston Rogers

Printed in the EU by SS Media Ltd

Contents

Career profiles

Has a degree in fine art and photography, and works as a
photography tutor at York College.

Has a degree in English and works as an education publishing
manager with English Heritage.

Has a degree in geography and works as an area environment
planning team leader with the Environment Agency.

Has a degree in archaeology and works as a custodian for a
property with the National Trust.

Has a degree in modern languages and is a self-employed
translator.

Has a degree in music and is a classical singer.

About the authors

Caroline Barker is a qualified careers practitioner with 20 years' experience of researching and writing in the fields of careers, education and training, including writing for the Connexions Direct jobs4u website.

Jenny Barron and Helen Evans are part of the in-house author team at Lifetime Publishing. They contribute to the widely used CLIPS careers information system and have authored a range of other student helpbooks and careers resources.

Acknowledgements

The figures quoted in Chapter five are reproduced with permission from *What Do Graduates Do? 2009'*, produced by the Higher Education Careers Services Unit (HECSU) and the Association of Graduate Careers Advisory Services (AGCAS). Source of raw data: HESA Destination of Leavers from Higher Education 2007/8.

Thanks to the graduates who were prepared to tell their stories for inclusion as profiles in this edition: Andrew Barker, Ffion George, Hilary Jones, Andrew Leigh, Tom Rodgers and Jenny Rust.

Thanks also to Philip Schofield, author of the previous editions of *Careers with an Arts or Humanities Degree*, upon which this edition is based.

Introduction

Whether you are thinking of studying for an arts or humanities degree, are already doing so, or have recently graduated and are unsure what to do next, then this book is for you!

Careers with an Arts or Humanities Degree aims to help you to choose the right subjects to study at A level or equivalent, assist you in choosing the degree course suited to you, and give you ideas about what you may want to pursue as a career.

Studying an arts or humanities subject/s can lead to a wide-ranging degree content and potentially diverse future career prospects, therefore you will have to research this area thoroughly. This book aims to equip you with the necessary tools and information in order to this.

Section 1 – Thinking about your future refers to what subjects you can study and the benefits of studying arts or humanities. You will look at what subjects you may want to choose, what your personal interests are, and help you choose the right study area and what you might want to do in the future. Chapter one looks at what subjects are covered within arts or humanities and the benefits of studying this area, whilst Chapter two is aimed at helping you choose your level 3 options. As you read on within Section one, you will begin to understand the subjects covered and the variety of courses and future careers available to you if you choose to undertake a career in arts or humanities.

The main arts and humanities subjects covered are:

- art and design
- English
- geography
- history
- languages
- media studies
- performing arts.

Section 2 – Careers using arts and humanities subjects looks at the careers in which you can make a direct use of your degree subject/s, although it is important to note that many of the careers dealt with in Section 2 are actually open to graduates of any discipline. Section 2 also carries case studies of arts and humanities graduates, who are now working in related careers and tell their stories, which we hope will help to inspire you.

Section 3 – Other careers you could consider highlights a range of other diverse career opportunities available to you as a graduate, irrespective of your degree subject.

We hope this book will broaden your awareness of the huge range of course and career options associated with the arts and humanities subjects, and will help you with your future career decision-making. Good luck!

Section 1
Thinking about your future

Chapter one

Why choose arts or humanities?

This chapter, aimed at those of you who have yet to choose your degree or other course beyond level 3, covers the following topics.

- What are the arts and humanities?

- Why study arts and humanities?

- Choosing a degree subject and course: things to consider such as personal interests; subjects and grades; types of courses

- The benefits of an arts and humanities degree

- Career prospects

What are the arts and humanities?

The subjects that form the basis of the arts and humanities are concerned with our histories, our arts, our cultures and our literatures. Typical AS/A level subjects you may be taking relating to arts and humanities (further outlined in Chapter two) include:

- art and design
- English
- history
- media studies
- languages
- performing arts
- geography.

When it comes to applying for university your choice of subjects in these areas opens up hugely – undergraduate degrees in the arts and humanities offer an unprecedented breadth of subject choice, from fine art and art history through to archaeology, cultural geography, linguistics and literature. There is a marvellous range of courses in subjects you've probably never met at school. You could choose to study anything from ancient civilisations to French literature or continental philosophy.

Why study arts and humanities?

There are many excellent reasons for taking a degree in the arts and humanities, including:

- because you are really interested in an arts or humanities subject for its own sake
- because you have a particular interest in a career area that it relates to
- because the skills you will develop are transferable to other careers
- because much of the graduate job market is open to graduates in these subjects.

Gaining an appreciation of the arts and humanities, whether it is in general terms or through the study of one individual academic area, helps us to understand our modern situations and challenges. In turn, then, arts and humanities degree subjects help us to approach problems, critically analyse them, and find solutions built on solid and well thought-out principles.

Choosing a degree subject and course

Which subject and particular course you choose to take can affect your future and therefore you will want to make the right decision. It is important therefore that you consider your options carefully in order to make an informed decision.

There are several things to think about when choosing a degree subject and then a particular course. These include:

- your personal interests and aptitudes

- your subjects and grades at GCSE – and more especially AS/A levels or their equivalents

- the types of courses available

- whether or not you have chosen a particular career or career path

- if undecided on your career, will your degree lead to skills in other career-related areas?

Personal interests and aptitudes

You may, like many people, choose a particular degree course because you have a particular interest in that subject and that it is something you want to pursue. Not only will this give you intellectual satisfaction, but your interest in the subject will help you to stay motivated throughout your studies.

When choosing a subject, bear in mind that your school experiences may not necessarily be a complete introduction to the particular subject you want to take at university or college. It is important therefore that you research courses and check their content thoroughly. Also remember that universities offer a huge range of courses. You may want to research other courses related to the subject you're interested in, or think about whether or not you want to combine subjects.

You need to consider your existing aptitudes – what you're currently good at. Most of us are better at subjects we like than at subjects we dislike, but not always. Don't assume that what you've done to date is all you can do, or what you could be best at. Don't underestimate your already developed skills and aptitudes! With an arts or humanities degree, you can develop new skills and aptitudes as well as fine tuning the ones you already have.

Your subjects and grades

The subjects you've taken at school will give you an idea of the areas of study that interest you, and your grades will tell you whether you've got an aptitude for them. Your choice of degree subject and course will be linked to your examination results at both A level and GCSE (or their equivalents). For example, some arts and humanities courses may require a specific AS/A level and relevant GCSEs (at grades A*-C).

You may also have relevant qualifications or aptitudes outside of school that may help you. For instance, you may be involved in a community arts project and have practical skills that could assist you in applying for a particular course. Remember that degree courses vary hugely, so it is well worth checking out specific entry requirements.

Types of courses

There are many choices of degree subjects and college courses covering the disciplines of arts and humanities. The range of single subjects or combined subjects is vast, so it is advisable to check out the course content, as different universities may have the same course or subject name, but their content can differ a lot.

All UK courses are listed in *Big Guide* published by UCAS. You should find a copy in your school/college of further education careers library, or in any good public reference library. You can also search courses through the UCAS website at www.ucas.com

More detailed information on choosing a higher education (HE) course is covered in Chapter two.

The benefits of an arts and humanities degree

The great thing about studying for an arts or humanities degree is that the wealth of courses available can set you up for a particular career path, or provide you with the necessary skills to adapt to any career market.

Future employers will look at your skills of analysis, critical thinking, communication and problem solving, all of which can be obtained through specific arts or humanities courses, or a combination of subjects. You may decide on a specific course for vocational reasons.

For example, you may choose a particular subject such as acting with a view to becoming an actor, or you may choose journalism with a view to becoming a journalist.

The thing to remember is that a particular quality of an arts or humanities degree is the all-round development of skills you will obtain. Whatever discipline, or combination of disciplines, you choose you will develop skills that are transferable to a whole host of related career paths.

You don't necessarily need to choose a degree course with a specific career in mind as you may change your views on this during your initial degree course. The main thing is to have an idea of your future career in mind; but be prepared that your feelings may change and that it is therefore good to keep your options open. With an arts or humanities degree, your options are wide ranging. The skills that you will develop during an arts or humanities degree can lead on to different careers such as business or teaching, but equally may be specifically linked to your chosen course such as fine art.

Career prospects

Many graduate vacancies are open to graduates with a degree in any discipline, and a lot of the skills learned on arts and humanities courses are very much in demand from employers. Many graduates are recruited for their intellectual skills – they know how to learn systematically, how to handle and interpret information, and how to analyse and solve problems. Employers also value the maturity, social skills and self-confidence that can come from three or more years of studying arts or humanities. So, for many people who haven't chosen their degree for vocational reasons, the value of studying for a degree is that it allows them to pursue an interest in a particular subject while developing skills that are valued by employers. They may then choose to specialise after their degree by taking one of the many vocational courses available at postgraduate level. See Chapter four for more information on postgraduate study options.

You can find out more about graduate careers in Sections 2 and 3 of this book. Section 2 covers graduate careers that relate to arts and humanities subjects, while Section 3 covers other careers you can consider.

Chapter two

Preparing for higher education

This chapter covers:

- choosing your level 3 subjects and courses – for those who have yet to choose their A level or equivalent courses

- choosing your higher education (HE) course – for those who have yet to choose their degree (or other course beyond level 3): things to consider such as different types of course; subject ideas

- the value of studying for an arts or humanities degree.

Choosing your level 3 subjects and courses

For most students, A levels remain the typical route into HE, but there are an increasing number of alternative pathways. The main arts- and humanities-related qualifications at advanced level (known as level 3) are outlined below.

A levels/Applied A levels

The main arts and humanities subjects to consider are **art and design, English, history, media studies, languages, performing arts and geography**. To that list you can add subjects such as **sociology, philosophy, business studies, social science, religious studies and theology**. Good grades at GCSE will be needed. Alternative routes of study are discussed later in this chapter.

If you're interested in undertaking arts or humanities at degree level, then many local education establishments may offer a humanities A level Pathway programme, which will be a combined AS/A level course combining many of the above subjects. This will stand you in good stead for studies at HE level. You will need to check with your local college/ sixth form to see what is available locally.

- There are also various other humanities-related AS/A levels that you could consider. However, not all schools and colleges offer these. As you may be less familiar with these subjects, they are described briefly below.

- **Anthropology** offers the opportunity to study today's society in terms of human interaction among cultures and the environment, identity and multiculturalism.

- **Archaeology** offers the opportunity to study aspects of science, art, technology, geography, sociology, history and religious studies through research into both historic and contemporary archaeological issues. This will also enable you to see how historic cultures influence modern-day society and the surrounding environment.

- **Citizenship studies** may appeal to you if you have a particular interest in communication skills, identity and how local, national and global politics can affect and influence citizenship issues.

- **Classical civilisation** offers the opportunity to gain a broad understanding of how Greek and Roman cultures have influenced Western theatre, art, literature and philosophy.

- **Critical thinking** looks at developing skills around decision making, as well as developing personal skills in preparation for HE and future careers.

- **Environmental studies** offers the chance to gain a broad understanding of the environment and to learn about the social and political aspects of environmental management. It has some topics in common with biology and geography.

- **Film studies** offers the chance to study the history of film and related industries, how films are promoted and received within modern society as well as the analysis of sound and imagery.

If you're thinking about taking arts and humanities subjects, it is very important that you **check entry requirements** to any HE courses that you are considering. **Many arts and humanities degree courses require one or more relevant subjects**, so you will need to consider your A level subject combinations carefully. Competition for arts and humanities degree courses is high, so you don't want to narrow down your options for HE courses, unless you are absolutely sure what you are ruling out!

Advanced Diplomas

Diploma qualifications, available in England, combine theoretical study with applied and practical learning about a broad area of work. Advanced Diploma qualifications are available in a variety of subject areas including creative and media, environmental and land-based studies, and travel and tourism.

BTEC National qualifications

BTEC courses also allow you to learn about an area of work. There is a range of BTEC National qualifications in art and design, media, languages, and performing arts and music. (N.B. By the end of 2010, these qualifications will be retitled as level 3 qualifications to fit into the new Qualifications and Credit Framework.)

Job-related qualifications

Qualifications that you gain when training in the workplace can lead to entry to certain HE courses related to that field of work. You could gain these through taking an Advanced Apprenticeship.

Access courses

Access courses in arts and humanities offer a route into HE, aimed particularly at those who have had some time away from education and do not hold the required HE entry qualifications. The Diploma in Foundation Studies in art and design, or art, design and media is one such course, but you would need to check with HE establishments to see whether this is acceptable as a stand-alone qualification, or whether it would need to be combined with other A levels or equivalent qualifications.

Choosing your subjects/course combinations

Entry to higher education

Entry requirements **for degree courses** are normally a minimum of either two A levels, a double-award applied A level, a BTEC National qualification, an Advanced Diploma or an equivalent qualification. You will also need supporting GCSEs, or equivalent. Often entry requirements are described in UCAS Tariff points. The Tariff is explained on the UCAS website and in *Big Guide*, published by UCAS. Many courses require more than the minimum stated above, and/or demand particular subjects. For example, A level art may be required, or subjects such as history, drama or geography. For some courses, BTEC National qualifications are only acceptable in combination with an A level in a particular subject. However, there are often great variations between HE institutions in entry requirements for the same degree subject. So it's worth doing your research!

Mix and match

One of the advantages of the range of level 3 qualifications on offer is that you can mix and match academic and vocational subjects. For example, it can be possible to combine a BTEC National qualification with an A level, or you could take an A level with an Advanced Diploma. Many people also choose a mixture of arts, humanities and sciences at A level, by studying a science alongside your chosen arts or humanities subjects. This can give you a more varied programme and will allow you insights into a different subject area. However, you need to be sure you are still taking enough arts or humanities subjects to keep your HE options open.

How many arts and humanities subjects?

Essentially the choice is up to you! Because arts and humanities is such a broad subject area, it is possible for you to combine a range of subjects such as English, art, history and a language. This would keep open the very widest choice of arts and humanities HE courses! However, you may have more of an idea about what you want to study at HE, so you might focus on a specific aspect of arts or humanities, such as performing arts, languages, or art and design. So, think about your interests and abilities, and take advice from your teachers, and again, check HE entry requirements.

Above all, when deciding on your subject combinations, you need to check that the combination of subjects and courses you finally choose are acceptable for entry to any degree or other HE course you may want to move on to.

So, research all the courses available in your area – not only in your school, if it has a sixth form, but also at local further education and sixth form colleges. You will be studying in much more depth than you have previously, so it makes sense to look at course content carefully, check whether the assessment methods would suit you and look at where the course could lead you. There is a lot to weigh up, but take advice from teachers and personal/careers advisers.

Choosing your higher education course

This section of the chapter is for all who are exploring their options for study at HE level.

All too many students drop out of HE because of a change of heart or because the course they chose did not meet their expectations, so do not rush into any decisions. Besides deciding which **subject** or subjects you are interested in studying, you will be faced with choices about the **type of course** to take.

Different types of course

The following is a brief overview of all the different levels and types of HE courses. As you will see, the HE qualifications available other than degrees are mainly offered in vocational (work-related) subjects, and take two years' full-time study.

First degrees

Degree courses (sometimes referred to as first degrees to differentiate them from higher or postgraduate degrees) are offered in a huge range of academic and vocational subjects. Degrees usually require three or four years of full-time study. Traditionally, first degrees are offered as single honours (study of a single subject) or joint or combined honours (two or more subjects are studied). Modular programmes, where students gradually build up their degree by taking individual units of study, offer the most flexibility.

For general information about entry qualifications for degree courses, look at the earlier section in this chapter, under 'Choosing your level 3 subjects and courses'.

Foundation year courses: some arts and humanities degrees may require an initial foundation year and are aimed at students without the usual entry requirements, such as those with non-related A levels. The year will bring the student's knowledge regarding arts or humanities up to a level where they can progress onto the first year of the degree. Increasingly, within arts and humanities, this is an optional qualification so it is well worth checking with the HE establishment first before applying.

Foundation degrees

Foundation degrees usually offer a mix of work-related skills and academic study. They are mainly offered in vocationally-related subjects, such as media and creative arts, and performing arts. They take two years, full time, and are also available through part-time or distance-learning routes – aimed at those in relevant employment.

There are no nationally-set entry requirements. Each institution sets its own entry criteria. The most important requirement is that you are capable of studying at HE level. Some institutions will ask for evidence of this, which could be previous study at A level or equivalent, an NVQ level 3, an Advanced Apprenticeship or completion of relevant work experience.

Higher National Diplomas and Certificates

Higher National Diplomas (HNDs) are also vocationally-related qualifications lasting two years, full time. They combine theory and practice, and prepare students for employment at differing levels.

Higher National Certificates (HNCs) are generally studied for on a part-time basis over two years, for people in relevant employment. However, there are a few full-time HNCs available, which take a year to complete.

Entry requirements to Higher National courses are flexible: admissions tutors may require one A level pass (often with a second subject studied to A level), a BTEC National qualification or possibly an NVQ level 3. If you have a vocational qualification it should be in a related subject area.

Diplomas of Higher Education

A Diploma of Higher Education (DipHE) is a qualification in its own right, normally awarded after completing the equivalent of two years of degree-level study. In terms of arts and humanities, there are courses available, particularly in art and design, and media. However, most DipHE courses are vocational, and entry requirements are often the same as for degree courses.

Other questions to ask yourself

- **Are you interested in a full-time, part-time or distance-learning course?** You might not have considered the idea of studying for HE on a part-time basis before. But many people do, and many earn while they learn. If the HE course is relevant to your job, your employer may contribute to course fees and allow you time off work to attend college or university. Others opt for the distance-learning option, such as through the Open University. For this approach, you need to be confident that you have the motivation to study independently.

- **Would you like to spend time getting work experience as part of your studies?** Some courses may offer a short work placement during the course. Alternatively, sandwich courses, as they are called, incorporate a longer period of work experience with an employer, generally lasting a year. If taking a degree, this usually takes place after the second year of study. Gaining such experience can prove beneficial when applying for jobs after your degree. See Chapter three for more information about the value of gaining work experience while you are studying.

- **Would you like to study in another country as part of your course?** Some four-year language courses offer a period in another country as part of the course. This is usually in the third year, either studying or, possibly, working with a specific company or within an educational setting. This time enables you to practise and improve your language/s of study, and can increase your confidence. Studying abroad may give you a head start if you are looking to work abroad in the future, for example in translation.

- **Are you considering progression from one level of course to another?** It is often possible to move from an HND to a degree course in a similar subject, or to top up a foundation degree to a full honours degree, with an extra year of study.

- **Are you interested in a subject you haven't studied before, but slightly unsure about taking it at HE level?** Most courses require you to study other related subjects at least for the first year, before you specialise in a particular subject. This gives you a chance to try out new subjects before narrowing down.

What to study

One big advantage of taking arts and humanities subjects at level 3 is that you will have a huge range of HE courses open to you. The downside is that this choice can be quite bewildering!

Generally, arts and humanities subjects fall under the seven main headings of **art and design, English, history, media studies, languages, performing arts and geography.**

If you are interested in one or more of these key areas, take some time to look at the course lists to get some idea about what is out there to help you make an informed decision about what you want to study.

Courses can be taken as single subjects or combined with other related subjects, such as art and design, drama and theatre studies, or geography with statistics. There are also combinations with unrelated subjects, like history with Spanish, dance with criminology, and media studies with geography.

What do you want to do after your HE course?

It is wise to look ahead and investigate the career options that will be open to you at the end of a course. Although some people begin HE with a definite career plan, they are in the minority. Most develop their skills, discover more about themselves and change their ideas as their studies progress. Lots change their minds about their original choice of course and about their career aims. Many are still undecided about their career direction even when they graduate.

Course ideas lists

Listed below are some **degree course** ideas, to act as a starting point for your research.

Make a list of the courses that interest you and find out more about them by viewing university websites and prospectuses. If there is a professional body that relates directly to the subject of interest to you, check whether they recognise or accredit any particular degree courses. Please note that the course lists are only intended as an ideas generator – they are by no means fully comprehensive. There are literally thousands of arts and humanities degree courses, and new subject combinations, new courses and new titles appear every year. You must get the most up-to-date information before you make your choice.

There are seven lists representing the main arts and humanities subjects. Whatever your interest, have a look through each list before choosing ones of interest, and then speak with your teachers, personal/careers advisers and HE establishments to find out more.

1. Courses related to art and design include

architectural design

applied art

art and design

art history

ceramics

clothing design

computer games art

contemporary furnishing design

decorative arts

digital arts

electronic media design

fashion design

fine art

fine art animation

graphic design

illustration

interior design

photography and video art

printed textiles design

public art

textiles art

theatre design

virtual reality design

2. Courses related to English include

English and business studies

English and creative writing

English and drama

English and film studies

English and geography

English and history

English and journalism

English language

English literature

English with media studies

English with teaching English as a foreign language (TEFL)

English with theatre studies

3. Courses related to history include

archaeology and ancient history

history and anthropology

history and art history

history and dance

history and geography

history and heritage

history with international politics

history and journalism

history and media studies

history and museum and gallery studies

history and music

modern and contemporary history

4. Courses related to media studies include

advertising with media studies

journalism and media studies

media and communication

media, culture and society

media, music and sound

media practices with public relations

media studies with digital imaging

media studies and drama

media studies with web design

photography, film and media studies

5. Courses related to languages include

Business and English as a foreign language

Chinese

English and Italian

French and linguistics

French and Spanish

German and global studies

Italian and politics

Japanese

modern language studies and philosophy

modern language studies with a year in Europe

Spanish and English

tourism management and Spanish

6. Courses related to the performing arts include

acting

arts and festivals management and dance

dance

dance and drama studies

drama

drama with film studies

drama theatre arts

media communications and music

music (performance)

performance and visual arts

performing arts (film, TV and stage)

popular music

7. Courses related to geography include

architectural design and geography

biology and geography

climate change and energy management

environmental geography

geographic information systems

geography with marine studies

geography and oceanography

geography and planning

geography and tourism

geology and geography

human geography and computing

third world development and geography

Please note...

Do not assume that a degree course automatically leads to a career in a certain area. For example, a degree in film does not automatically lead to a career as a film producer or director!

Many of the above subjects can be studied in combination with other subjects, including non-arts and humanities related subjects, such as arts and applied mathematics, drama studies and biology, and performance arts and psychology. So whatever degree course you choose arts and humanities degrees can provide you with the necessary knowledge and skills for a diverse employment market.

The value of studying for an arts or humanities degree

There are many benefits of gaining degree-level qualifications. Whatever your subject, studying for a degree will:

- give you the opportunity to study a subject of interest to you up to a high level
- open up a wider range of career opportunities for you
- help you to develop a range of skills valued by employers
- increase your future earning potential
- provide you with the chance to make new friends from a range of backgrounds, and opportunities to develop new interests
- give you an experience you will always value.

An **arts or humanities degree** has particular benefits.

An arts or humanities degree gives you valuable skills

Arts and humanities covers a diverse range of subjects, many of which can be combined and is often seen as an 'all rounder' area of study. As a result, an arts or humanities degree will help you to develop creative, team-working, communication, presentation, decision-making, critical-thinking and problem-solving skills.

An arts or humanities degree opens doors

A degree in any of the arts or humanities disciplines is a starting point for a lot of different career routes: as well as job areas where a specific degree is essential or where related knowledge is an advantage, arts and humanities graduates can enter the range of career areas that are open to graduates of any discipline (described in Section 3). This is due to the diversity of key skills you will develop during your degree, which can be easily transferred to a whole host of careers.

A variety of career pathways will be open to you

Graduating with an arts or humanities degree can lead you towards a dynamic career with so many career pathways available to you. Depending on which discipline you choose, you could find yourself pursuing a career in the performing arts, as a musician or an actor; a career within the media, such as media design or broadcasting; or be undertaking research into future planning requirements having graduated with a geography degree. The thing to remember about arts and humanities is that there are many careers you could choose, and the skills you learn along the way are transferrable into many career pathways.

As well as the aforementioned careers, you may want to consider a wider use of your degree, such as marketing and public relations, arts administration, advertising or teaching. There are so many opportunities for you to look at. Don't just think about specific careers related to your chosen degree – think about your skills, as well as other careers that may be related to your degree and are of interest to you!

You may find that you start out on one career path and then use your knowledge and experience to change to another later in your working life. With an arts or humanities degree, the choice of career is wide ranging and constantly changing, meaning there are more options for your chosen career!

Working it out

This chapter is just a starting point. There are many other things to be done before you can reach a decision about what to do in HE. There are new ideas to consider, people to talk to and other sources of help and information to explore.

What help can you get?

- Use the careers information and guidance resources listed in Section 4. They may be available in your school, college or careers centre/Connexions service library.

- Talk to your teachers.

- Read more about the courses on offer through the UCAS website, in course prospectuses and university websites, and in HE handbooks. Widen your knowledge through magazines, quality newspapers, relevant books, visits, lectures, open days and 'taster' courses at universities.

- Visit the websites of relevant institutions.

- Talk to your personal/careers adviser.

- Talk to someone who has completed a course that you are interested in, if you can.

- Investigate the websites of employers that may interest you.

- Try some work experience or holiday jobs.

- Discuss your thoughts with family and friends.

It is most important that you find out what the courses that interest you are about, particularly if you have not studied the subjects at level 3. Don't just assume that you know: make sure you understand what is involved.

Consider the stage you are at now, and decide where you are in your career planning. If you need a professional qualification to get into the career of your choice, check that the courses you are considering are accredited by a relevant professional body if necessary. The more you find out, the more your interests will clarify and new ideas will grow. Make sure that you choose the course that will suit you best, because that will lead to success in your studies and the best chance of a career you will enjoy.

Chapter three

Preparing for your career

This chapter discusses ways in which you can improve your employability, and start preparing for your career, while you are still an undergraduate. It covers:

- work experience

- supplementary skills you can develop alongside your degree

- boosting your CV through your extra-curricular activities

- the careers services available to you.

To gain a degree in any subject is a notable achievement. However, on its own, a degree is unlikely to land you the job of your dreams. When it comes to finding work, you are going to find yourself competing with others who may be similarly, or even more highly, qualified. So what can you do to give yourself an edge? The following describes ways in which you can prepare for your career while still a student, by adding value to your degree.

Work experience

Undertaking work experience while you are a student takes planning and motivation, but it offers significant benefits and will be looked upon favourably by future employers. The most beneficial option is to find work experience that is relevant to your course and future career ambitions, although any work undertaken as a sideline to your studies can still prove useful. In general, it allows you to:

- gain practical, hands-on experience that shows you can apply your academic studies to the 'real world'

- get an insight into the range of jobs available to you – what they involve and their potential progression routes

- 'try out' an employer to see if you like them

- start building a network of contacts

- develop an understanding of the 'world of work', which will eventually help you to settle into a permanent role more easily

- potentially gain a future referee, to use when applying for jobs after your degree

- possibly earn some money!

Don't forget – work experience also lets an employer 'try you out' to see if they like you! Employers are increasingly using work experience placements as an extended 'interview' for places on their graduate training schemes or for other permanent roles further down the line.

Degrees with built-in work experience

If you have yet to select your degree course, you could think about choosing one that incorporates work experience. **Sandwich courses** typically last for four years and combine full-time study with one or more industrial placements, i.e. supervised, practical experience and training with an employer. Look into how closely connected your higher education (HE) institution is with key employers in the industry and how much help you will receive in finding placements. Note also that **foundation degrees** and **HNDs** offer a high level of work-based learning, and can be 'topped up' to a full degree with further study.

Internships

Also known as summer placements, vacation schemes, work experience and so on, **undergraduate internships** offer a fixed period of employment during your vacation. They are usually offered to students in their penultimate or final year of studies.

If it's not long until you graduate, or you have just done so, a **graduate internship** may be worth considering. As for other types of work experience, they can help make you more employable, or they may offer a stop-gap if you are struggling to find a permanent position.

The number of internships is on the increase. Major employers often see them as a means of selecting the best candidates for permanent positions on their graduate training schemes. Others may offer them with a specific short-term project in mind. In recent times, the Government has also been encouraging employers to take on graduate interns as a means of addressing unemployment among young people. Not all internships offer paid employment, however; in some cases you will only be paid expenses.

Competition for places can be fierce, so it is worth doing your research well in advance to find out what's available and exactly when and how you need to apply. Employers usually follow a formal application process, expecting you to apply in writing, attend an interview and, possibly, undertake tests at an assessment centre. They may also set criteria regarding your grades: for example, only accepting candidates who have achieved, or are predicted to achieve, at least a 2.2 degree award.

Most HE institutions provide support to students looking for internships. Ask at your institution's careers service or placement office, or look for information in the library. The *Student Guide to Work Experience* may be available from such sources; alternatively it is available to purchase for a small charge from the National Council for Work Experience. See www.work-experience.org for further details, and for a list of companies that have been accredited for the quality of their work experience placements.

Many major employers run internship programmes, including P&G, GSK, Centrica, BP, Cancer Research and so on. However, don't overlook the opportunities available with smaller employers. For example, the Shell *Step* programme matches undergraduates to small and medium-sized companies and community organisations for paid, project-based work placements. See www.shellstep.org.uk for full details.

There are various organisations that can help students from under-represented groups find internships. For example, EmployAbility works primarily with disabled students, see www.employ-ability.org.uk. Some employers also target under-represented groups. The Civil Service is an example of such an employer; it offers *Summer Diversity Internship* programmes aimed at disabled students and students from black and ethnic minority backgrounds. For more information, visit www.civilservice.gov.uk/summerdiversity.

You can search online for internships with a wide range of employers via the Prospects website at www.prospects.ac.uk/workexperience.

N.B. At the time of writing the Department for Business, Innovation and Skills is running the *Graduate Talent Pool* scheme. This is an online vacancy service, which allows recent graduates to search and apply for internships. It is not yet known whether this will be an ongoing scheme; it is currently limited to applicants who graduated in 2008 or 2009. See www.direct.gov.uk/graduatetalentpool for further details.

Supplementary skills

Most degree courses will help you develop a range of transferable skills, such as team working, time management and so on. While employers certainly value these 'soft' skills, they may also look for ability in other, more practical, areas such as languages and ICT.

You are likely to have the opportunity to develop such skills at your HE institution, through:

- course modules that can be taken alongside your main studies

- evening classes, often at a discounted price

- self-study – e.g. through access to a language or IT centre and its resources.

Language skills are obviously useful if you want to work or study abroad, but also if you want to work in the UK for an organisation with international connections. Most HE institutions offer a wide range of modern foreign languages; think about which languages could be of most benefit to your situation.

You are also likely to be able to develop your **ICT skills**, not only in the specific technologies that relate to your field of study, but also in generic applications, such as wordprocessing, spreadsheet, database, presentation, image manipulation and web-related packages.

As an induction to most degree courses, you are likely to be offered help in developing your **research and information skills**. This is likely to include how to use the web effectively, perform literature searches and make full use of library resources. Such skills are critical to achieving your degree, but also have many applications in the workplace.

You may be surprised at what else may be on offer – short courses to develop your **enterprise skills**, **get published**, or learn how to **touch type** or **drive**; sessions with **guest speakers** and much more! Contact your student support service for further information.

Extracurricular activities

The HE isn't just about studying! There are many clubs and societies you can join at most institutions, which can offer a welcome break from academia. While these offer a chance to indulge your passions, or develop new ones, they can also enhance your CV in the eyes of a potential employer.

Think of all the transferable skills you can gain from being a member of a sports team, debating society, drama club, music group, college radio station or Students Union entertainment team! Potential employers will be able to use this as evidence that you are team player, or even a natural leader, and that you are skilled at organisation, negotiation and promotion, for example. In the absence of work experience, being able to demonstrate these skills from other areas of your life will be vital. Showing that you have a healthy work/life balance may also be important.

Other options may include joining an Armed Forces university unit or undertaking voluntary work, the Duke of Edinburgh's Award programme, Young Enterprise Graduate Programme or other scheme that shows evidence of personal development.

Careers services

Higher education institutions are very keen to see their students find suitable employment after graduation, so tend to offer a great deal of support in this respect. They may offer a careers service not only to current students, but also to those who have already graduated, although possibly for a limited amount of time only. Typical support includes one-to-one guidance sessions, workshops, careers events and access to a variety of resources. You can use these services to find out about your options, clarify you career aspirations, practise applications and interviews, take aptitude tests, research employers and vacancies, investigate postgraduate study options or get advice about starting your own business.

Careers fairs and the 'milk round'

Careers fairs, organised by HE institutions, tend to take place in the autumn and spring terms and give you the opportunity to meet with potential employers. These may be major, national organisations as well as smaller, local employers. Such fairs may be seen by employers as a chance for them to 'sell' themselves to you!

The '**milk round**' is the informal name for the season of recruitment fairs that enable employers to start looking for potential graduate recruits. They may be organised by the HE institution careers service or, occasionally, by independent organisations that stage them in exhibition centres open to students from any HE institution. In general, recruitment fairs have been on the decline in recent times, partly because of the economic downturn, but also because of the rise in internet recruitment.

Employers that attend recruitment fairs tend to be the major, 'blue chip' companies that are looking to recruit to their formal graduate training schemes. Although you are very unlikely to be offered a position there and then, such encounters are still an important part of the recruitment process and should be approached as such! Research the employers that are of interest to you, take your CV, dress appropriately and be prepared to meet with managers and other key staff who will have some influence over your eventual recruitment. If possible, take contact details and follow up with employers after the event when you make your formal application.

Seize the day!

For many people, studying for a degree is a once in a lifetime opportunity and it's common to look back on those exciting few years – and wonder where the time went! So it makes sense to exploit your time in HE to the full. Gaining a degree is just part of the experience; if you can also start preparing for your future career in the ways described above, it will be time very well spent!

Chapter four

Postgraduate study options

This chapter covers:

- the benefits of postgraduate study
- the different types of postgraduate study
- funding postgraduate study
- postgraduate study abroad.

What are the benefits of postgraduate study?

A postgraduate course can not only broaden your knowledge and skills, or allow you to pursue your interest in a subject, but can also open up new career opportunities. There is a huge range of postgraduate courses on offer in arts and humanities subjects leading to many different careers. The beauty of a vocational postgraduate course is that it gives you a chance to specialise in a particular vocational area. This is ideal if you've taken a broad-based, non-vocational course at first degree level and then decided to pursue a particular career goal.

For some career areas, such as teaching and law, you'll need a professional qualification. For others, a postgraduate qualification may not be essential but will definitely increase your job prospects, especially in highly competitive sectors. You'll need to research the career area you're interested in to find out how relevant (and they are becoming increasingly relevant) a postgraduate qualification may be.

You can read further about entry requirements to different careers relating to arts and humanities in Section 2, which will give you an idea of some of the careers for which a postgraduate qualification is highly recommended. For example:

- to work as a curator you'll normally need a postgraduate qualification in museum studies

- taking a relevant postgraduate course will definitely boost your prospects of entering translating and interpreting work

- the majority of trainees in the newspaper industry are recruited after taking a full-time vocational course

- to become an archivist you need a postgraduate qualification recognised by the Society of Archivists.

What is postgraduate study?

Postgraduate study is study that graduates take to gain a masters or doctoral degree, or a postgraduate diploma or certificate. Depending on the degree taken, study may be through a taught programme or through a research programme.

Taught programmes

- **Masters degrees** – masters degrees have different titles according to the subject and method of study. Master of Arts (MA) and Master of Letters (MLitt) are both used for a range of arts and humanities subjects. Programmes normally last 12 months full time or two years part time. They may be available as conversion courses to develop your skills in a new subject, such as business or IT, or be vocational courses that lead to a professional qualification.

- **Postgraduate diplomas/certificates** – these courses are often vocational and include professional training, such as the Postgraduate Certificate in Education (PGCE) required to teach, or a conversion course such as the Graduate Diploma in Law (GDL). They usually last nine months full time or two years part time. You may be able to upgrade your diploma to a masters degree.

If you have a relevant first degree then you can enter many careers by taking a masters degree or postgraduate diploma accredited by a professional body. Geography graduates, for example, could become town planners by taking a masters degree accredited by the Royal Town Planning Institute (RTPI); or become land surveyors by taking a postgraduate qualification accredited by the Royal Institution of Chartered Surveyors (RICS).

If you enter work as a graduate, then you may still go on to take further study. In many jobs you will be encouraged to take a relevant postgraduate course part time while working. This will be part of your ongoing professional development.

Research programmes

- **Master of Philosophy (MPhil)** usually signifies a masters degree obtained by research, in any subject. Research masters degrees involve the in-depth study of a defined subject over a period of at least one year. You are likely to receive training in research skills, and work independently to prepare a thesis. Many graduates begin a research masters degree with the intention of upgrading it to a PhD.

- **Doctor of Philosophy (PhD)** is the highest level of academic qualification. The title of PhD is used across the full range of academic subjects. It involves at least three years of supervised research resulting in a thesis. Within arts and humanities subjects you will probably need to gain a masters degree before embarking on a PhD.

Many humanities graduates choose to take a PhD purely because of their interest in the subject, others take one as a route into an academic career. A PhD is essential for entry into an academic career due to the competition for posts.

Funding issues: where will the money come from?

You'll need to think about how to fund your postgraduate study. Unfortunately this is a problem for thousands of students because there simply isn't much funding available. One thing to note is that the money won't come from the Student Loans Company (which provides financial help for new full-time HE students). Unless you intend to study for a PGCE you will not be eligible for a student loan! You may need to work part time, or take time out to work before you begin postgraduate study, to raise funds for it.

You may be able to get funding from public funding bodies, such as the Research Councils, through universities and colleges, and from charitable organisations and trusts. You could also apply to a bank for a Professional and Career Development Loan of up to £10,000, which you pay back after you've stopped studying. For more information visit www.direct.gov.uk/pcdl.

The Arts and Humanities Research Council (AHRC) promotes and supports research and related postgraduate training in the arts and humanities. You can download their *Research Funding Guide* on their website at www.ahrc.ac.uk. To be eligible for a full Research Council award you'll normally need a first-class (1:1) or upper-second class (2:1) honours degree from a UK HE institute, be an EU national and have been resident in the UK for the three years before your application.

Postgraduate study abroad

Opportunities to study abroad are increasing, with literally thousands of universities overseas offering taught masters and research degrees. You may be attracted to the experience you'll gain spending time in a new country or by the opportunity to work with specialists in your field. Whatever your reasons for choosing postgraduate study abroad the range of courses is huge – from studying fashion marketing management in Italy to studying climate change in Denmark – and you'll certainly find one to suit your area of interest.

You will, however, need to research courses carefully. The range and quality of study available can differ widely from country to country. Course titles, content, entry requirements, length and funding can also vary. You'll need to check whether your existing qualifications are acceptable and think about how you are going to fit into another culture. Above all, studying abroad will involve a high level of personal commitment, as well as consideration of financial issues, so you'll need to think through all the options and practicalities carefully before you make a decision.

Chapter five

Graduate destinations

This chapter may be useful if you are thinking about undertaking a degree in arts or humanities, or are already taking one, and would like to know how other graduates in this area have got on in the world of work. It covers:

- graduate destinations
- starting salaries
- international options.

While no one knows exactly what the future may bring, it can still be useful to look at what other people in similar situations have achieved as a way of looking at what you may want to do. It can help you set your own expectations on a realistic level, or may encourage you to be a high flyer and outperform everyone else!

However, you cannot control all the factors that may impact on your future career, such as the state of the economy, vacancies, market trends and so on. Often, being in the right place at the right time is down to luck rather than judgement!

The following figures are from an annual survey and show the destination of students six months after they graduated in 2008. [The figures shown in the tables below and in the sections relating to employment destinations and starting salaries are reproduced with permission from 'What Do Graduates Do? 2009', produced by the Higher Education Careers Services Unit (HECSU) and the Association of Graduate Careers Advisory Services (AGCAS). Source of raw data: HESA Destination of Leavers from Higher Education 2007/8.]

	Broad subject area						All subjects
	art & design	English	history	media studies	languages	performing arts	
No. of graduates in 2008	16,135	11,060	10,380	5,735	8,380	9,795	276,930
No. of survey respondents	12,570	8,620	8,135	4,340	6,620	7,635	220,065
Employed	65%	54%	52%	68%	55%	62%	61%
Undertaking further study or training	7%	21%	22%	7%	21%	15%	14%
Working and studying	5%	8%	7%	4%	7%	7%	8%
Unemployed	12%	8%	10%	12%	8%	8%	8%
Other	11%	9%	10%	10%	9%	8%	9%

Figures from '*What Do Graduates Do? 2009*' – see acknowledgements.

Note: percentages have been rounded up.

While looking at the above figures, it is important to remember that the graduates of 2008 would have been entering the job market in a time of economic recession. It is interesting to see that arts and humanities graduates had similar rates of unemployment to most other graduates. However, in the case of art and design, history and media studies unemployment was higher than most other graduates with an average of 11% unemployed six months after graduating. Still, as the economy moves out of recession, the percentage of those unemployed should start to decrease as employers begin to recruit once more, so don't let this put you off unnecessarily!

Further study or training

Looking at the previous table, it is also clear to see that graduates of English, history and languages are more likely than other graduates to go into a period of further study or training, with over a fifth of graduates in these subjects electing to pursue this route.

A further breakdown of figures, relating to students undertaking further study or training six months after graduating, shows:

	Broad subject area						All subjects
	art & design	English	history	media studies	languages	performing arts	
Studying in the UK for a higher degree	3.4%	9.6%	11.8%	3.7%	8.7%	6.1%	6.6%
Studying in the UK for a teaching qualification	1.6%	6.4%	3.6%	1.2%	5.1%	4.4%	2.5%
Undertaking other further study or training in the UK	1.9%	5.1%	6.1%	1.6%	5.8%	3.8%	4.7%
Undertaking further study or training overseas	0.1%	0.3%	0.3%	0.0%	0.9%	0.2%	0.2%
Total of all respondents	7%	21.4%	21.8%	6.5%	20.5%	14.5%	14%

Figures from 'What Do Graduates Do? 2009' – see acknowledgements.

From these figures, it is clear to see how common it is for graduates of English, history and languages to go on to study for higher degrees, i.e. masters degrees and doctorates. Also, the percentage of English and languages graduates who go on to teacher training is more than double the percentage of many other graduates. And, although small in overall terms, the percentage of languages graduates who go to study or train overseas is nearly five times that of other students. It may seem obvious that a graduate of languages may go on to study or train overseas, but this is still a significant figure compared to most other graduates.

Employment

Of those graduates who were employed in the six months after graduating, their typical jobs varied very much according to their degree subject.

Of art and design graduates in employment:

- 31% worked as **arts, design, culture and sports professionals**, such as broadcasting, fashion design and commercial art

- 15% worked in **other occupations**, including art class assistants.

Of English graduates in employment:

- 10% worked as **educational professionals**, such as secondary teachers and TEFL (Teaching English as a Foreign Language)

- 9% as **commercial, industrial and public sector managers**, including graduate traineeships

- 7% as **arts, design, culture and sports professionals**, including newspaper reporters.

Of history graduates in employment:

- 9% worked as **business and financial professionals and associate professionals**, such as chartered accountants, internal auditors and recruitment consultants

- 11% as **commercial, industrial and public sector managers**

- 5% as **other professionals, associate professional and technical occupations**, such as researchers.

Of media studies graduates in employment:

- 17% worked as **arts, design, culture and sports professionals**, including television production assistants, broadcasters and magazine editors

- 9% as **marketing, sales and advertising professionals**

- 10% as **commercial, industrial and public sector managers**.

Of languages graduates in employment:

- 12% worked as **business and financial professionals and associate professionals**, such as management consultants, conference, exhibition and events coordinators and consultants

- 12% as **commercial, industrial and public sector managers**

- 7% as **arts, design, culture and sports professionals**, including journalists and translators.

Of performing arts graduates in employment:

- 24% worked as **arts, design, culture and sports professionals,** including actors, stage and studio managers, and musicians

- 13% as **educational professionals,** such as dance tutors and drama teachers.

Note: percentages have been rounded up.

Source: *What Do Graduates Do? 2009* (see acknowledgments).

As well as the above graduate courses in arts and humanities, you may well be looking at embarking on a degree in geography.

As with the above graduates, those of you looking for careers using a geography degree will face the same issues regarding vacancies, job market trends and the impact of coming out of economic recession.

The information below details the destinations of students with a geography degree, six months after their graduation.

	Broad subject area	All subjects
	geography	
No. of graduates in 2008	2815	276,930
No. of survey respondents	2280	220,065
Employed	58%	61%
Undertaking further study or training	19%	14%
Working and studying	7%	8%
Unemployed	6%	8%
Other	10%	9%

Note: percentages have been rounded up.

Figures from *'What Do Graduates Do? 2009'* – see acknowledgements.

From the above figures, it is clear to see that the percentage of people undertaking further study or training is higher than most other graduates, and is a comparable figure to English, history and languages graduates. Also, the percentage of those employed following their graduation is slightly lower than, but similar to, most other graduates, and this is consistent with the overall trend of other graduates with an arts or humanities degree. It is important to bear in mind that the overall number of graduates with a geography degree is much lower than those who graduated with other arts or humanities degrees, but the overall trend is similar.

Further study or training – geography graduates

Looking at the previous table, it is also clear to see the comparisons with graduates of English, history and languages, with around one fifth of geography graduates electing to pursue the route of further study or training.

A further breakdown of figures, relating to students undertaking further study or training six months after graduating, shows:

	Broad subject area	All subjects
	geography	
Studying in the UK for a higher degree	10.6%	6.6%
Studying in the UK for a teaching qualification	4.2%	2.5%
Undertaking other further study or training in the UK	4.0%	4.7%
Undertaking further study or training overseas	0.2%	0.2%
Total of all respondents	**18.2%**	**14%**

Figures from *'What Do Graduates Do? 2009'* – see acknowledgements.

From these figures, it is clear to see how common it is for graduates of geography, as well as English, history and languages, to go on to study for higher degrees, i.e. masters degrees and doctorates. Also, the percentage of geography graduates who move into undertaking teaching qualifications is relatively high compared to most other graduates, but is in comparison with English and languages graduates.

Employment – geography graduates

Of those graduates who were employed in the six months after graduating, their typical jobs varied very much according to their degree subject.

Of geography graduates in employment:

- 13% were employed as **business and financial professionals and associate professionals**, such as assistant management accountants, business development consultants and actuaries

- 10% as **other professionals, associate professional and technical occupations**, such as geographical information system (GIS) advisers, graduate transport consultants and graduate hydrographic surveyors

- 15% as **commercial, industrial and public sector managers**, including National Graduate Development Programme trainees.

Note: percentages have been rounded up.

Source: *What Do Graduates Do? 2009* (see acknowledgments).

Starting salaries

Starting salaries[1] for all students graduating in 2008 and entering into full-time work, ranged from £14,000-16,000 for those in administrative work and customer services, to an average of £25,362 for those in health professions such as dentists, doctors and psychologists. Across all occupations, the average salary six months after graduating was £19,677.

For those graduating with an arts or creative arts degree, average salaries ranged from £14,843 for fine arts, to £16,469 in design-related employment.

For those students who graduated with a humanities-related degree, salaries varied from £16,295 (media studies) to £16,642 (English studies). Students who graduated with a geography degree had an average salary of £18,664, while those graduating with a European languages degree saw average starting salaries of £19,000.

It is important to remember that salaries vary depending on who you work for and the location of the job. For instance, people working in London traditionally earn higher salaries, which reflects a higher cost of living, but this does not mean that similarly salaried jobs are not available elsewhere.

Whatever your starting salary, remember that as a graduate you have significant potential for progression over the course of your career. Your ultimate salary will depend on your commitment to your chosen career and to your continuing professional development (CPD), as well as your performance, self-promotion and overall ambition!

---

[1]Figures from '*What Do Graduates Do? 2009*'

International options

With a degree in arts or humanities, there may well be opportunities to pursue further study or employment abroad. You may have already spent time abroad as part of your studies, particularly if you did a language degree, and want to pursue this further, or you could be looking at working for a multinational company.

Although only a small percentage of graduates actually progress to further studies or working abroad, it is important to remember that these opportunities are available. Possible routes into employment generally include working as a translator, or Teaching English as a Foreign Language (TEFL). Other options may be linked to research opportunities, especially in geography-related subjects and multimedia design.

Don't forget that UK nationals can live and work in any European Union (EU) country, but if you choose to look at opportunities outside the EU, then you will usually require a visa or work permit.

Another way of gaining experience abroad would be to undertake a period of volunteering. Voluntary Service Overseas (VSO) offers volunteering opportunities around the world in a variety of settings, concentrating on humanitarian issues. This would enable you to enhance your skills and gain valuable experience in a different environment, and could lead to employment or training opportunities. For further information, visit www.vso.org.uk.

If you do choose to look at volunteering, working or continuing your studies abroad, make sure you research the job or course thoroughly, and ensure you familiarise yourself with the culture of the country you are considering. Find out more at www.prospects.ac.uk.

Section 2
Careers using arts and humanities subjects

Chapter six

Careers using art and design

This chapter covers the following careers in the visual arts sector:

- artist (including illustration and art therapy work)
- design work
- photographer.

The chapter includes a career profile of a fine art and photography graduate working in education.

Visual arts is a vibrant sector that also acts as a feeder to other industries such as design, advertising, interactive media, film publishing and the games industry. The sector covers individual artists, publicly-funded institutions, museums, galleries, studios, arts fairs, arts centres, education bodies and festivals. Freelancers and sole traders, many of whom manage portfolio careers moving between commercial and not-for-profit activities, dominate the sector. People working in a wide range of professional roles, including for example technicians, educators, curators, publicists and agents, support the art world.

Artist

Artists create original work, such as paintings, sculptures and installations. They then try to sell their work, through agents, dealers and galleries. Artists create their work in many ways, including: painting, photography, computer-aided digital art, video, etching, printing, sculpting and carving.

Most artists are self-employed. Sometimes artists are commissioned to produce a one-off piece of work. An artist may also work with an organisation such as a school, hospital or prison, as an artist in residence, developing work for a collection or an exhibition, or teaching and running workshops. Many artists also contribute to education programmes and work on public or community projects.

Your work may involve:

- buying and storing media and materials for use
- developing and maintaining a portfolio of work to show to clients and galleries
- promoting your work to dealers, agents and galleries
- developing a website or brochure for promotion and showcasing work
- planning, organising and working for an exhibition
- managing and maintaining a studio or other work space
- participating in a range of promotional activities, such as open studios, to promote and sell work.

It is extremely difficult for artists to make their entire living from selling their work, and therefore you will probably need to supplement your income through other activities, such as teaching art.

Fine artists work not only in contemporary art, but also in other career areas like film, publishing, video and arts administration, where the value of art training is increasingly recognised.

Many artists work as illustrators – developing ideas and producing original visual images for a wide range of products, including novels, textbooks and technical manuals, advertising materials, magazines and newspapers, television and film animations and storyboards, computer games, websites and mobile phone visuals. Illustrators combine art, design and creative skills. This type of work overlaps with that of graphic designers.

Many artists teach, which means getting a postgraduate teaching qualification. Some artists work as **art therapists** in homes for people with learning difficulties, in hospices with the terminally ill and in psychiatric hospitals. They help withdrawn patients to express themselves through painting and other forms of art. This helps to relieve patients' tensions and can provide psychiatrists with valuable clues to patients' problems from the work produced. To do this sort of work you must have completed an art therapy training course at masters level, which would take either two years full time, or three years part time. Art therapists, once qualified, need to undertake continuing professional development (CPD), as it is a mandatory condition for renewing state registration.

Design work

Design work can be categorised into two broad categories: two-dimensional and three-dimensional. Two-dimensional design is concerned with visual communication using flat surfaces, and includes graphic and textile design. Three-dimensional design concerns the design of solid shapes – from cars to jewellery, CD players to ceramics, and stage sets to furniture.

Two-dimensional design

As a two-dimensional designer you may work on graphic design, which includes typography (choosing and designing the layout of lettering), illustration (including photography) and the design of company symbols (logos). You may be employed by a design agency or as part of an in-house team. Organisations requiring design work on a frequent basis often have their own artists and designers. You could work freelance, but this is only advisable after some experience in employment. Areas in which graphic designers and commercial artists are employed include the following.

Advertising

Designing posters; advertisements for newspapers and magazines; TV, web and film commercials; product packaging; display cards etc.

Book publishing

Designing dust jackets and covers, typography, illustration (including technical illustration and photography), designing book catalogues and promotional material.

Periodical publishing

Designing covers, choosing illustrations and photographs (and sometimes creating them), typography and designing page layouts.

Multimedia publishing

Illustrating text with visual images, sound, animation, film and video clips for CD-ROMs and DVDs.

Website design

Designing websites; using logic trees to help users find the information they are seeking; and illustrating text with visual images, animation and other devices.

TV, film and video

Designing opening titles, credits, animation sequences and other graphics.

Image consultancy

Designing logos and corporate 'liveries' for big organisations. This may include everything from the stationery to colour schemes for shops, offices and company vehicles.

Textile manufacturing

Designing fabrics (using patterns, colours, weaves, fibre mixtures) for garments, bedding, carpets, soft furnishings, and so on.

Three-dimensional design

You will work in one of four main areas – craft, interior, product and fashion design – each with its own specialisations.

Craft work

Craft work involves designing and producing both decorative and utilitarian items such as jewellery, silverware, handmade furniture, ceramics and glassware (including stained glass). You might work in craft workshops, designing individual, handmade or unique objects. Alternatively, you could work in craft manufacture, producing designs or prototypes for similar objects but with the intention of mass production.

Interior design

Interior design is concerned with the use, furnishing and decoration of interior spaces. Interior designers must be aware of how people use space. For example, when designing an exhibition in a museum or gallery, the designer must take into account the flow of people past the exhibits and the views they will get. They must also be aware of any safety or security aspects and of legal requirements in the design, especially in public or commercial interiors.

Interior design work falls into four main categories.

- Consultancy – designing interiors for ships, aircraft, hotels and other industrial, commercial and domestic buildings; also managing contracts to ensure that the work is done on time and as specified.

- Theatre, TV and film – designing sets; can involve historical research into details of architecture, furnishings, etc.

- Exhibition organisers – designing stands, usually involving collaboration with graphic designers and advertising or marketing specialists.

- Museums – designing gallery layout and special exhibitions.

- Retail stores – designing window and 'point of sale' displays.

Product design

Product design is concerned with manufactured goods such as cars, china, furniture, computers, DVD players, light fittings, mobile phones, machine tools and thousands of other products. This involves close collaboration with design engineers, production engineers and other technical specialists, as well as with marketing people who understand customer likes and dislikes. Designers in this field have to know a lot about the characteristics of materials (both in manufacturing and then in how the product is being used) and production methods.

Fashion design

Fashion design, which includes footwear, covers everything from haute couture to garments and shoes for mass production. Areas of employment include the following.

- Haute couture – fashion houses that design exclusive 'model' garments. Only one or two copies of each design are made, almost entirely by hand.

- Wholesale couture – similar to haute couture, but several copies of each original are made for sale through selected retail outlets.

- Wholesale manufacturing – designing clothes for mass production. Most designers specialise, for example, in childrenswear, men's suits, sportswear, knitwear, footwear, accessories and so on. Designs may follow trends set by the haute couturiers or could be based on 'classic' lines. The clothes produced will range from inexpensive, seasonally-changing fashion items to longer-lasting quality goods.

- Film, TV and theatre costume design – can involve historical research as well as design. You may be required to adapt previous costumes as well as designing completely new items.

Photographer

Professional photographers create permanent, visual images that communicate a specific message to the viewer. Their purpose may be artistic, commercial or editorial. They may work in fashion, advertising or editorial photography, high street shops or studios, in newspapers, in medical photography, and in TV, film and radio. The electronic revolution has given photography a boost, adding fast and exciting image-making tools, and competition in this sector is vigorous.

Typically your work may involve:

- choosing and preparing locations

- setting up lighting

- selecting appropriate cameras, lenses, film and accessories

- setting the aperture and shutter speed

- composing pictures

- image manipulation using software packages such as Photoshop.

Photographers usually work to a brief set by the client. The brief may be very detailed, or it may allow the photographer scope for creative interpretation of the client's ideas, after appropriate consultation.

Rates of pay will depend on your experience and reputation, the type of shoot and the budget available. The hours can be long and unpredictable, and you'll need to be prepared for periods where there may be little or no work. Success depends on steadily building up a business and gaining a reputation, which can lead to more regular work and higher fees.

Tom Rodgers

Tom describes his career path into teaching, his role as a photography tutor and his plans for the future in terms of developing his career and his work as an artist.

Career profile

Job title: photography tutor

Employer: York College

Post-16 qualifications: A levels in art and English language, AS levels in maths and general studies

Degree: BA fine art and photography

Postgraduate qualification: Post-Baccalaureate Certificate in fine art

After my degree, my first job was at a comprehensive school where I worked as an arts technician. I also had a job as a substitute art teacher in various prisons. I then moved to America for a year to undertake postgraduate study at the School of the Museum of Fine Arts in Boston. On returning to the UK, I went back to the prisons while I looked for work that would develop my career. It was at this point that I contacted York College who were in need of a photography tutor.

The move into teaching was prompted by the need for money and a desire to remain involved with art subjects. Working in educational establishments also enables me to be in constant contact with the subjects I love and to be surrounded by fresh ideas and enthusiasm. The position in the prisons made me realise that teaching is an incredibly rewarding and inspirational profession.

In my current job I am responsible for the management and administrative running of A level photography at York College. I also plan and design the overall course structure, while sharing the teaching and more detailed planning with a colleague. I teach approximately three to four days a week and also take care of open events, parents evenings and other extracurricular activities.

The main qualities needed in this profession are largely interpersonal skills. A good deal of the contact I have with students is based on individual discussions, which require self-expression from the students and empathy from the tutors. Recognising each student's individual abilities, which must be nurtured and developed, is very important. You also need a teaching qualification – I am currently in the second year of a Postgraduate Certificate in Education.

A great deal of work, research and planning needs to be done outside class time to accommodate each student's needs, as they all have different questions and are all working on an individual piece of work. Perhaps the main challenge is keeping everything organised while retaining the ability to have breaks and personal time outside college.

The one thing that really makes me feel good is seeing work of great skill coming from the students. I am always surprised by how creative and talented they can be. I believe that learning in a creative environment not only teaches the subject at hand but also how to engage with the world and how to react in an appropriate manner. It is immensely rewarding to see my students mature into highly expressive and creative young adults.

My plans for the future will hopefully see developments for my career and my work as an artist. I hope to continue working at York College to get as much experience as I can in teaching in further education. However, I would like to move into teaching in higher education and in order to do this I will need an MA. Should both of these happen I will, I feel, have the chance to develop my own work through contact with students and colleagues who are also working at a high level of skill and accomplishment.

Entry qualifications

While there are no formal qualifications to enter visual art and design work, it is becoming increasingly difficult to enter without a relevant degree or vocational qualification. For example, entry into professional interior design usually requires a relevant degree or HND, and fashion designers usually start their career after taking a degree or HND in fashion.

There is a huge range of undergraduate degree courses available. Which one you choose will depend on your areas of interest and whether or not you want to take a general or more vocational course. Courses range, for example, from:

- general art and design courses

- specific courses in all areas of design, including fashion, graphic, interior, etc

- specific art-related courses, from fine art to illustration and animation

- courses in digital media and photography

- combined courses in all areas, for example fine art photography.

Courses vary in their entrance requirements. Admissions tutors will expect evidence of creative talent in a portfolio of your work. Many students take a one-year foundation course to help them progress to higher education. This comprises an intensive year of introductory study to many art and design areas and may include drawing, painting, printmaking, sculpture, photography, video, computer design, textiles, fashion, ceramics and three-dimensional design.

If you intend to become a practising artist, then you should also consider taking a postgraduate teaching qualification so that you can supplement your earnings by teaching. Apart from having an exceptional talent, you'll also need to be resilient and flexible.

To be a designer your talent must be supplemented with an ability to work in a team and willingness, at times, to compromise your artistic standards to meet the constraints of costs, simplicity of manufacture and other factors.

Artists and designers are by nature creative problem solvers and lateral thinkers. If you're thinking of freelancing you'll also need good communication skills to build contacts, excellent self-motivation to complete work on time, and the ability to accept criticism and rejection.

Training and career development

As an artist you are largely responsible for your own development. You may choose to continue taking classes and to establish contact with fellow artists. Networking is important, not just to promote work, but to reflect and learn from others and receive feedback. Artists often collaborate with other artists in community work or for joint exhibitions.

In design, training of graduates is primarily on the job, working alongside experienced designers. The Chartered Society of Designers offers a structured programme of continuous professional development.

You are likely to start as an assistant of some kind. As an assistant you may initially work mainly in a supporting role, involved in routine typography, producing working drawings for a product from a designer's rough sketch, designing simple components or researching materials for someone else's design proposals. Further progress will depend on your performance, not only in creative terms but also as a member of a team creating a product, whether it be advertising material, a knitwear design or manufactured goods.

Finding vacancies

Openings in advertising are most likely to be found in *Campaign*, *Marketing* and *Marketing Week*. Also check the website of the Institute of Practitioners in Advertising (IPA). Look for vacancies within publishing in *The Bookseller*, *Publishing News*, and the national press. Illustrators and designers should look in *The Guardian* on Saturdays, *Creative Review* and *Design Week*. Also check recruitment websites, including those of employment agencies, and specialist websites such as www.careersindesign.com.

Sources of further information

Arts Council England – tel: 0845 300 6200. www.artscouncil.org.uk and www.yourcreativefuture.org.uk

Association of Illustrators – tel: 020 7613 4328. www.theaoi.com

British Association of Art Therapists – tel: 020 7686 4216. www.baat.org

British Institute of Interior Design – tel: 020 7349 0800. www.biid.org.uk

Chartered Society of Designers – tel: 020 7357 8088. www.csd.org.uk

Crafts Council – tel: 020 7806 2500. www.craftscouncil.org.uk

Creative & Cultural Skills – the Sector Skills Council for crafts, cultural heritage, design, literature, music, performing and visual arts. Tel: 020 7015 1800. www.ccskills.org.uk and www.creative-choices.co.uk

Design Council – tel: 020 7420 5200. www.designcouncil.org.uk

National Society for Education in Art and Design – tel: 01225 810134. www.nsead.org

Skillset – the Sector Skills Council covering the advertising industry. Helpline: 08080 300 900 (England and N. Ireland) or 0800 012 1815 (Wales). www.skillset.org/careers

Chapter seven

Careers using communication, media and film

This chapter covers the following career areas:

- advertising – including account executive, copywriter and media buyer
- film – including runner and film director
- public relations work.

Advertising

Advertising is broadly concerned with promoting and selling products and services. It is a creative and fast-paced industry that is always in need of talented individuals and fresh ideas. Increasingly, campaigns are carried across different media, such as print, billboard, digital communication, TV and radio. There are several different types of advertising agencies including:

- integrated agencies, offering clients the whole range of advertising advice and creative services
- media agencies, which specialise in buying advertising space
- digital agencies, which focus on online marketing
- direct mail and direct marketing agencies.

Account executive

An account executive looks after a group of clients in an advertising agency and is in almost daily contact with them. As an account executive, you are the link between the agency and the client throughout advertising campaigns. You must get the best possible work on behalf of your client, from your colleagues in other departments and your suppliers – copywriters, art directors, media executives, researchers and administrators.

Typically your work will involve meeting your client to discuss their advertising requirements; working with colleagues to devise an advertising campaign that meets the client's brief and budget; briefing media, creative and research staff; liaising with the client throughout; and managing campaign costs. Account executives usually report to the account manager.

The account executive's job is to keep clients happy and it can be very stressful. However, you'll certainly be offered plenty of intellectual and management challenges. Being an account executive is also one of the best routes to top management in advertising.

Entry qualifications

Entrants usually have a degree. Advertising is a very competitive sector to enter and subjects such as advertising, marketing, communications and English may increase your chances. Work experience at agencies in summer holidays will help you to gain contacts and strengthen your application. Some of the larger agencies offer formal work experience/ internship programmes – more details are available on the Institute of Practitioners in Advertising (IPA) website at www.ipa.co.uk.

You'll need to have a genuine passion for advertising. You'll also need to be a team player and be able to form strong working relationships, as well as being able to work under pressure.

Training and career development

Training is mainly on the job. Some of the larger agencies run graduate training schemes. As a junior account executive you may take the IPA Foundation Certificate, which covers the entire brand communication process.

If you aim to develop your long-term career in advertising, there is a range of professional qualifications available through the Communication, Advertising and Marketing Education Foundation (CAM), the IPA and the Chartered Institute of Marketing (CIM).

Quick promotion can be guaranteed for those who shine. With experience you may progress to account manager, account director and eventually group account director.

Copywriter

Copywriters are employed in advertising agencies to write advertising, TV and radio commercials, and other promotional materials for clients. Some are also used by corporate communications companies to write brochures and annual reports. It is a disciplined form of writing.

To write good copy, you must understand the characteristics of the product and what will motivate your audience to buy it. You need imagination to find new ways of saying things that have been said scores of times before, and to catch and hold the public's interest. And you should be aware of prevailing fashions in order to keep your ideas one step ahead of the trend.

You must work well with other people, especially clients, creative directors and designers. Copywriters for TV commercials tend to be specialists who can think in visual terms and work closely with a producer. Brochure writers too are often specialists.

Entry qualifications

Copywriting doesn't require any formal qualifications, although it is normal to have a degree. As key requirements are creativity and the ability to write well, subjects such as English, journalism, communications, media studies, advertising and public relations may improve your chances. Copywriting courses are also available, many by distance learning. Many copywriting entrants have worked in journalism, marketing or sales.

You will need to be a fluent, imaginative and disciplined writer. You must have an interest in helping businesses to achieve commercial success. You'll need to be a good team worker and be able to work to tight deadlines.

A common route in is by compiling a portfolio of advertisements you've written and getting it critiqued by advertising agencies.

Training and career development

Advertising agencies don't have trainee schemes for copywriters. You learn on the job. Your progress as a copywriter will depend on the success of the campaigns you work on. This will be reflected in your salary and your reputation in the industry. The best copywriters are very highly paid. Career development is often achieved by moving between agencies. Many successful copywriters go freelance or set up their own agency. Some end up heading international advertising groups.

Media buyer

Media buyers mainly work in media agencies. They recommend the best medium, or mix of media, in which to place a particular advertisement or advertising campaign, and then buy the space or time on behalf of the client.

As a media buyer you have to weigh up the respective merits of different newspapers, periodicals, radio and television stations, cinemas, poster sites, websites and so on, in terms of their potential to reach the client's target audience. You'll draw on circulation figures; readership, listening and viewing surveys; and many other statistical sources. You need an analytical mind and the ability to express the statistical data in lay terms.

You also buy time or space from media owners. Advertising rates are often open to discussion, especially if you are buying in volume, so you should also have a taste for negotiation. Graduates are often found on the other side, selling advertising space or time on behalf of media owners. Much of this is done via the telephone direct to advertisers. However, with large advertisers and with agencies the selling is usually carried out face to face.

Entry qualifications

Entry is competitive and entrants usually have a degree. Subjects such as media studies, business studies, statistics, marketing and communications may increase your chances. As for account executives, mentioned earlier, work experience is valuable.

You'll need excellent teamwork and communication skills. You'll also need good numerical, analytical and research skills; a good understanding of the media; and commercial awareness.

Training and career development

Many of the larger agencies run structured training programmes. Training is mainly on the job, joining a team of senior planners and buyers. Training courses are available from industry bodies such as the Media Research Group (MRG), the IPA and Media Circle.

Media buying is fast moving and there are good opportunities for career progression. With experience, you may progress to media manager and then media director.

Finding vacancies

Jobs in advertising are published in *Campaign*, *Marketing*, *Marketing Week* and *Media Week*. Also on the IPA website (see below), the Chartered Institute of Marketing (CIM) website (see below), as well as in the national press. Many agencies advertise jobs on their websites or through specialist recruitment agencies such as the Drum and Revolution.

A speculative application to someone you'd like to work for, if you've researched the agency thoroughly, can win you an interview and many advertising jobs are found this way. The IPA has a list of agency members on its website.

Sources of further information

CAM Foundation – tel: 01628 427120. www.camfoundation.com

Chartered Institute of Marketing – tel: 01628 427120. www.cim.co.uk

Institute of Practitioners in Advertising – tel: 020 7235 7020. www.ipa.co.uk

Media Circle – tel: 0207 367 6981. www.mediacircle.org

Media Research Group – www.mrg.org.uk

Skillset – the Sector Skills Council covering the advertsing industry. Helpline: 08080 300 900 (England and N. Ireland) or 0800 012 1815 (Wales). www.skillset.org/careers

Film

The film industry is divided into five sectors:

- development – the writing, packaging and financing of film ideas and scripts

- production – the process of setting up and shooting scenes in a film

- post-production – where the shots are assembled, treated and mixed into a finished product

- distribution – the process of selling the product to audiences, via cinemas, retailers and rental firms

- exhibition – the cinemas that screen the film for the general public.

The UK film industry is constantly evolving. Due to the nature of the industry production companies are often set up for a specific production and then close down after production is complete, therefore it is difficult to gauge the number of companies in the film industry at any one time. There are production companies, distribution companies and exhibition companies. The UK industry is an independent creator of feature films, a co-production partner and a provider of services to the international film industry.

There are hundreds of jobs within the film industry, each one requiring a unique set of specialist skills. The majority of these roles are found within the film production sector. Production crews are divided into departmental hierarchies, with each department having set tasks at each stage of the production process. You can find detailed information on careers in the film and other creative media industries on Skillset's website at www.skillset.org/careers .

Runner

The role of runner is recognised as a key entry-level position for a career in the film production sector. Runners provide essential support in every area of production. You would be working within the production department doing all kinds of tasks in order to help everything run smoothly. You would report to a producer, director or editor.

Typically your work would involve:

- fetching and delivering items such as tapes and scripts
- transporting crews between locations
- looking after visitors
- general administrative work
- making teas, coffees and lunches
- keeping the set clean and tidy
- carrying out basic research
- hiring props and ordering stock.

On big-budget features there may be several runners, each assigned to a different area such as sound, camera, art department and editing. On shorter films, runners get the opportunity to work across all areas of production, from initial office planning, through to principal photography, to clearing up or assisting with post-production.

You'll be working long and unpredictable hours, and may be required to work some nights and weekends. Freelance and short-term contracts are common.

Entry requirements

Competition is intense for this role. There are no set entry requirements, but a degree or foundation degree in film or TV production may be an advantage. Other courses that may be useful include degrees in media and broadcasting skills, multimedia, and drama and theatre. Courses with a practical focus may increase your chances. Relevant work experience is essential, and you may need to do a significant amount of unpaid work experience to get into the industry.

Skillset's network of Screen Academies consists of institutions that have been approved as centres of excellence in education and training for film. Details are available on its website, which also has a comprehensive course database.

You'll need enthusiasm and energy, excellent communication and networking skills, together with flexibility and the ability to think on your feet, as well as a genuine passion for film and TV. You'll also need a full, clean driving licence and your own transport.

Training and career development

You'll learn a wide variety of new skills on the job and also gain a broad insight into all areas of the industry. Runners progress by establishing a good reputation and strong contacts. In the film industry most runners start in the production office. They may then become more senior there, and progress to production coordinator/production manager careers. Alternatively they may become a floor runner (studio and location). Work as a floor runner can open the door to third-, second- and then first-assistant director roles, or establish connections to other departments.

Finding vacancies

Some vacancies may be found on www.productionbase.co.uk and www.mandy.com. Runner positions, however, are rarely advertised so networking is a vital skill to develop. Approaching companies directly can be a way in. Develop a portfolio, soundreel or showreel of your work, for example film shorts, radio recordings or photographs that will illustrate your talent to companies, along with an impressive CV. Entering competitions and showcasing your work at festivals may also be a way to get yourself noticed. Check industry directories, such as

The Knowledge and PACT, for contact details and credits of companies before approaching them. The Production Guild is also a useful source of information.

Film director

Directors are responsible for the creative vision and overall style of a film. They act as a vital link between the production, technical and creative teams. They translate the film's written script into actual images and sounds on the screen. Throughout this process they are supported by a number of assistant directors. They need to work within the constraints of the film's budget and schedule.

Directors may write the film's script or commission it to be written. They then develop a vision for the finished film. They need to elect the right cast, crew and locations for the film. Once the film is in production they direct rehearsals and other performances of the actors. They also manage the technical aspects of filming, such as the sound, camera, lighting, design and special-effects departments. Directors also work closely with editors throughout the post-production stage, to reach the final version of the film.

Entry requirements

There are no formal qualifications to become a director. Directing your own short film or an amateur play, or writing a screenplay, may help. Valuable practical experience can also be gained by working on student productions or in community media. However, in-depth industry experience is vital for this role, as directors need an extensive understanding of the entire filmmaking process. Many directors work their way up from entry-level positions such as a runner.

See 'Runner' (above) for courses that may be useful as a starting point. There are also specialist postgraduate courses in directing available. Entry requirements vary and applicants should check with individual institutions, but most will expect applicants to have a showreel of work and ideas for future projects or scripts.

You'll need to have artistic vision and creative skills, confident leadership skills, be able to think clearly under pressure, have a great determination to succeed, together with commitment and a deep passion for filmmaking.

Training and career development

Directors develop their skills through in-depth practical experience. They also need to keep up to date with filmmaking techniques and equipment.

There is a wide range of short specialist courses available – from working with actors to multicamera directing techniques – through regional screen agencies, training companies and film schools.

You'll need to establish a reputation through a successful body of work in order to continue to secure work. Some directors set up their own independent production companies.

Finding vacancies

You may find vacancies on specialist industry websites such as www.productionbase.co.uk but many directors find out about work opportunities through personal industry contacts. Some directors are represented by agents.

Sources of further information

British Film Institute (BFI) – tel: 020 7255 1444. www.bfi.org.uk

Directors UK – tel: 020 7240 0009. www.directorsuk.com

Film and Television Freelance Training (FT2) – tel: 020 7407 0344. www.ft2.org.uk

New Producers Alliance – tel: 020 7613 0440. www.npa.org.uk

Shooting People: Independent Filmmakers Network – shootingpeople.org

Skillset – the Sector Skills Council covering the advertsing industry. Helpline: 08080 300 900 (England and N. Ireland) or 0800 012 1815 (Wales). www.skillset.org/careers

UK Film Council – tel: 020 7861 7861. www.ukfilmcouncil.org.uk

Public relations work

The aim of public relations (PR) is to manage the reputation and image of an organisation or, sometimes, an individual. The job focuses on developing and maintaining good relationships with everyone whose support and goodwill are essential to the client's success.

Public relations specialists are used by all kinds of people and organisations: commercial and industrial firms, central and local government, universities, celebrities, charities, politicians, public services, trade and professional bodies, and environmental and other pressure groups. Some organisations have their own public relations departments; others use PR agencies that act on their behalf.

Public relations staff provide stories about their client or organisation and its products where appropriate. These stories have to have news value if they are going to be used by the media – so finding new and novel angles is a major challenge. Most of the information is issued through press releases, press conferences, brochures, websites, the annual report and house magazines. Your work will bring you into close contact with journalists. You might even ghost write speeches and articles for a client's executives.

As you can see, PR work is varied. The range of your duties will depend on where you work. In-house departments vary in the scope of their activities: they may divide their work between internal staff and external experts. Some agencies specialise in one area of PR work, such as corporate communications, while others handle all aspects of PR. However, typically your work will include going to client briefings and other meetings, making presentations, attending press conferences and writing material for public or press information.

Entry qualifications

Public relations is increasingly becoming a graduate-entry career. Many PR officers have a degree, which could be in public relations or other subjects such as communications, marketing, journalism, media studies or English. Some entrants to the profession transfer from journalism.

The Chartered Institute of Public Relations (CIPR) lists CIPR-approved degrees and postgraduate degree courses in public relations on its website. These are specialised programmes, which will provide you with relevant theoretical and practical skills, and may help to improve your chances of employment in a fiercely competitive marketplace.

You'll need excellent communication, interpersonal and writing skills; creativity and imagination; and to be able to remain calm under pressure. You'll also be expected to have a good knowledge of current affairs.

Training and career development

Training is normally on the job, working with a senior colleague or manager. The CIPR runs a wide range of training programmes, as well as continuing professional development (CPD). They also offer CIPR professional PR qualifications, which are industry approved, including:

- Advanced Certificate – for graduates and candidates in the early stages of their career

- CIPR Diploma – for more experienced practitioners who want to develop their strategic PR management skills.

Job titles vary a lot. An in-house PR officer may progress to PR manager and then PR director.

Finding vacancies

The CIPR runs a PR Jobshop on its website (at www.ciprjobs.co.uk) listing current job vacancies. You will also find PR vacancies advertised in the magazine *PR Week* and on its website at www.prweekjobs.com. Also look out for opportunities with those organisations that have their own public affairs or public relations departments.

Sources of further information

Chartered Institute of Public Relations – tel: 020 7766 3333. www.cipr.co.uk

Chapter eight

Careers using English

"It's best not to put LOL!!! and OMG!!! in company reports."

This chapter focuses on the publishing, broadcasting and UK press industries and covers the following careers:

- book publishing – including commissioning editor, copy-editor and other functions

- journalism – including newspaper, magazine and broadcast journalism.

The chapter includes a career profile of an English graduate working in a publishing role.

Book publishing

Some people thought that electronic media would replace book publishing. However, although customers are accessing media increasingly via mobile phones, e-books and websites, the book is still hugely popular. The UK book publishing industry alone published around 120,000 new or revised books in 2008 and sold over 850 million books. Electronic publishing is growing rapidly and many publishers are actively involved, with the sales of e-books predicted to rise and strengthen the industry.

The main functions in book publishing are:

- editorial
- design and production
- marketing (including sales, public relations and publicity)
- distribution
- contracts and rights
- administration (including accounts and computing).

We will concentrate here on the editorial function as this is the area where your English degree is likely to be most relevant. Some of the other functions may offer a way to start in the publishing industry, with the possibility of moving into editorial work later, and are looked at briefly.

Commissioning editor

Commissioning editors find new books to publish. Publishing is a business like any other and must make profits to survive. It is the role of the commissioning editor to know what will sell in their market and to obtain manuscripts accordingly. They do this by following trends in the book market in order to know what readers want. They may do this by looking at market research surveys, liaising with marketing and sales staff, and attending book fairs.

Literary agents acting on behalf of authors usually send the manuscripts of unpublished books to publishers. Authors also send in unsolicited manuscripts themselves, but an enormous number of these are rejected. Commissioning editors decide which manuscripts to accept or reject. They may also employ readers to assist in selecting books for publication.

Many publishers, particularly of technical or educational books, specifically order or commission books to be written. Once a need for a work on a particular subject has been identified, the commissioning editor will find an expert or experts to write it. The commissioning editor will agree the contents of the manuscript, and when it must be delivered, with the author. The editor will also negotiate fees, advanced payment and royalties with the author and arrange for the contract to be drawn up. They would then monitor the progress of the book until it is published.

Copy-editor

Supporting the work of commissioning editors (and managing editors) are copy-editors (text is called copy), desk-editors or sub-editors. Their function is to read the manuscript and prepare it for setting. They check manuscripts for logical structure, accuracy, clarity and the effective use of language. They cut repetitive statements and contradictions and correct errors of spelling, grammar and punctuation. Extensive revisions are sometimes needed. All these must be discussed and agreed with the author. Editors must be good with people if they are to get the best out of their writers.

Once edited, copy goes to design and production to be turned into a printed book. Illustrations may be chosen or commissioned, involving discussion between the author, artist and editor. Authors supply their manuscripts on a disk or as an email attachment. An editor will therefore often work on screen so it is important to have good wordprocessing skills. There is an increasing move towards using freelance staff in publishing. Freelance copy-editors usually move into such work after several years' experience within a publishing house.

Other functions

Experience of other functions makes good preparation for an editorial career. Jobs in marketing or rights are especially useful. Working in these areas will develop an awareness of what is required of a book if it is going to sell. You will also be in contact with authors.

Sales and marketing

This area covers all the activities necessary to promote and sell books. Publicity staff produce advertising, press releases, book lists and other materials. They also run special events such as lecture tours and arrange appearances by authors on TV and radio chat shows to promote their latest book. Sales staff sell the books to the wholesale and retail book trade, to specialist library suppliers, or direct to end customers such as schools or colleges. Marketing employs more people than editorial and production combined.

Contracts and rights

Staff in this department handle the legal side of publishing. They cover the initial agreements and contracts with authors and any issues arising from further developments of a book, such as translation or the sale of film or serial rights.

Entry qualifications

Editorial work in book publishing is normally a career for graduates and competition for posts is high. You'll need a good knowledge of English grammar and be able to demonstrate a genuine interest in books. If you hope to join a publisher in such specialist fields as science, medicine or art history, you will need an interest in and some knowledge of the field. You also need to have a meticulous eye for detail and be well organised. A modern foreign language is required in some international publishing houses. There are an increasing number of postgraduate qualifications (as well as some undergraduate degrees) related to publishing. While employers do not specify these qualifications as essential, they may help your application stand out and provide you with work experience and networking opportunities.

Training and career development

As an initial entrant you are likely to be recruited in a junior post such as an editorial assistant, or you may join a publishing house in any job you can get and then apply for an editorial vacancy when one arises. Training normally takes place on the job, although larger publishers may have structured training programmes. The Publishing Training Centre and the Society for Editors and Proofreaders run courses including topics such as copy-editing and proofreading.

In large publishing companies progression is usually through the ranks, from a junior editorial role to senior commissioning editor. Commissioning editors may progress into general management or may choose to become self-employed, either as a literary agent or by setting up their own publishing company.

Finding vacancies

General publishing vacancies can be found in the national press, the main trade magazine *The Bookseller* (online at www.thebookseller.com), and on the websites of publishing companies. There are also specialist recruitment agencies, such as Inspired Selection, that advertise a wide range of editorial jobs.

Further information

London School of Publishing – tel: 020 7221 3399.
www.publishing-school.co.uk

Skillset – the Sector Skills Council for creative media. Tel: 080 8030 0900. www.skillset.org

Society for Editors and Proofreaders – tel: 020 8785 5617.
www.sfep.org.uk

The Publishers Association – tel: 020 7691 9191.
www.publishers.org.uk

The Publishing Training Centre – tel: 020 8874 2718.
www.train4publishing.co.uk

Hilary Jones

Hilary outlines her route into her current role within publishing, and the responsibilities in her job as an education publishing manager.

Career profile

Job title: education publishing manager

Employer: English Heritage

Post-16 qualifications: A levels in English, history and French

Degree: BA English

Postgraduate qualification: MA English literature

During my degree I knew I wanted to do anything related to publishing but really didn't give too much thought to my career. Looking back, I would advise anyone studying English and interested in publishing to try to get some vacation work experience, or take some relevant short courses, for example with the Publishing Training Centre.

After my degree, personal circumstances meant I was living in an area with limited opportunities in this field so I first got a job as a youth information worker. I then went on to take my masters degree and really applied myself on the course, which was totally useful as I learned valuable practical editorial and proofreading skills.

After the course I moved to Bath and started applying for editorial work. After a stint as a sales assistant and trainee revenues officer (obviously not my chosen careers!) I got a job with Lifetime Publishing as an author. During this time I was writing careers leaflets and books aimed at young people, and gained valuable project management experience. I then spent a short time working as a research executive in an advertising agency. I had this idea it would be glamorous, but it didn't match my expectations and I decided I wanted to go back into publishing.

I then moved to my present job with English Heritage. As the education publishing manager I am responsible for education resources. This includes putting together Heritage Learning, a free twice-yearly magazine for teachers that includes teaching activities across all Key Stages of the National Curriculum. This involves, for example, picking different themes for each issue (the last one was sustainability), identifying and commissioning authors, editing articles, image research and supplying articles to the designer.

I also inherited a huge back catalogue of published material. I'm looking through this material in terms of what is still relevant and can be updated as useful resources for teachers, which will be freely available online. I also look after the education pages for the website, researching and writing the content, and supply pictures and articles for Engaging Places, another online teaching resource, which supports teaching and learning through buildings and places.

You need project management skills in this job, people management skills (I currently have a volunteer working for me) and tenacity. You also need specific editorial skills such as proofreading.

I like everything about my job! It's really diverse as I'm the only person within the Education Department who is responsible for the written work. The main challenges are juggling all the projects I'm working on and meeting deadlines, which can be stressful. I'm not sure what I'd like to go on to do in the future. To be honest, I'm not really thinking about this as I'm very happy where I am right now!

Journalism

Journalists collect and disseminate information. They keep the public informed about news and current affairs. Work is available in two main areas: broadcasting and the press. The press can be further subdivided into press (or news) agencies, and newspapers and periodicals.

Within broadcasting, there is a wide range of areas available in **broadcast journalism**. The main areas are:

- radio
- television
- online communications
- online news bulletins
- current affairs
- magazine programmes.

Broadcast journalists investigate and report on news and current affairs. They may work as editors, reporters, presenters, producers and correspondents. Some also work as researchers on documentary programmes.

Press (or news) agencies feed news to other media. The most famous news agencies are the Press Association and Reuters. Agencies provide objective information for other journalists to use. The work of news agencies is especially useful in those situations where other media representatives may not be present. This might include war zones, where journalists from specific countries have been excluded for political reasons.

The **UK press** is made up of 125 daily and Sunday newspapers, about 800 weekly newspapers and some 1,000 weekly local free papers. There are also around 6,000 magazine titles, ranging from glossy magazines to trade newsletters. Many publishers also produce material in new media, for example CD, web or audio, in addition to hard copy. Newspaper journalists are also increasingly writing stories for publication on newspaper websites.

It's probably worth checking out the annual *Willings Press Guide* that can be found in most reference libraries. This lists every newspaper and magazine (be it consumer and special interest, or business and professional) published in the UK. Each entry gives information on the publisher, address, telephone, fax numbers, website and frequency of publication.

Journalists can develop as specialist reporters or correspondents. National papers have journalists who specialise in a particular subject. On other papers, and in news agencies, they usually mix general reporting with one or more specialisms. Specialist areas include, for example, travel, sport, entertainment, motoring, business, foreign news, science and technology, education and health.

Entry qualifications

You don't necessarily need any qualifications to enter journalism other than your degree. However, competition for places is tough, and a vocational qualification in journalism will definitely give you an advantage. In fact, the majority of trainees in the newspaper industry are recruited after attending a full-time vocational (pre-entry) course and most recruitment into broadcast journalism is via a Broadcast Journalism Training Council (BJTC) accredited course (see below).

You must be able to write factual, concise and clear English. The emphasis in journalism is on accuracy, clarity, brevity and speed. An interest in current affairs and a good general knowledge are essential. Having physical and mental stamina is important, because the job can involve a lot of travel and irregular hours. Reporters in newspapers, radio and TV often work evenings and weekends; shift working is common on daily newspapers and in broadcasting.

To be a radio or television journalist you also need a good speaking voice. To enter periodical publishing it is also helpful if you have a good knowledge of the subject covered by the magazine you want to join. Experience on a student or community publication is valuable. It is also useful to have had a work experience placement on a newspaper.

Training and career development

Newspaper journalism

There are two routes into newspaper journalism – direct entry and pre-entry via college/university courses, described below.

- **Direct entry** – if you have been recruited into the industry from school or university, you will be regarded as a direct entrant. Most companies will expect you to enter into a two-year training contract during which time you will receive basic training. Most companies will register you with the National Council for the Training of Journalists (NCTJ) and provide you with a distance-learning foundation course to study. After about six months you should ideally attend a block-release or day-release course at college, during which time you will sit the NCTJ's preliminary series of examinations. Following a further period of employment, you will have the opportunity to obtain the NCTJ's National Certificate.

- **Pre-entry via college/university courses** – if you are recruited into the industry after attending a full-time vocational training course then this route is known as pre-entry. Journalism courses accredited by the NCTJ range from undergraduate degrees to masters degrees and postgraduate diplomas. You'll probably enter into an 18-month training contract and, as with direct entrants, you will be expected to obtain the NCTJ's National Certificate. Accredited courses can be found on the NCJT website (see below). Some of the courses are for graduates only, and include fast-track postgraduate courses lasting up to 24 weeks. Courses that are not accredited by the NCTJ have little credibility in the industry.

Almost every journalist starts as a trainee reporter, usually on a regional daily or local weekly newspaper. They cover everything: local council meetings and court cases, fires and floods, accidents, political demonstrations, sports events and interviews with visiting celebrities.

In newspapers there is no set career structure. You may for a time head specialist parts of the paper, such as the City or women's pages. You may become a news editor, allocating stories to individual reporters and attending editorial conferences. You may become a sub-editor. As a sub-editor you'd work on stories fed in by reporters, often rewriting opening paragraphs, cutting for length and giving stories an angle. You'd also write the headlines.

If you want to reach senior posts (such as deputy editor and editor) where you have control over the content of a whole publication, you'll need to have been a sub-editor and probably have headed a number of specialist sections.

Magazine journalism

Training in magazine journalism is less formal than in newspapers. Many graduates enter in junior positions and receive training that varies from informal learning from others while on the job, through to a structured programme of development. However, there are a number of colleges and universities offering courses that are accredited by either the NCTJ or by the Periodicals Training Council (PTC) for graduates wishing to enter the magazine industry. These include 19-week fast-track diploma courses and one-year masters degrees or postgraduate diplomas in magazine journalism. Currently accredited courses are listed on the Periodical Publishers Association (PPA) website and the NCTJ website (see below).

The three main branches of magazine journalism are news writing, feature writing and sub-editing. There is no fixed career path in magazine journalism, but magazines do offer the opportunity to get on fast if you've got talent. You may progress from staff writer to sub-editor, section head and chief editor, or you may move into newspapers, TV journalism or public relations.

Broadcast journalism

All the main employers in broadcast journalism – including the BBC, ITV and Sky – support the BJTC. The Council currently accredits nearly 50 courses in colleges and universities. Many BJTC-accredited courses are full-time postgraduate courses lasting a year. There are also a number of undergraduate degrees in broadcast journalism. Look up the BJTC website (www.bjtc.org.uk) for an up-to-date list of these courses.

Broadcast journalists who start in TV often begin as newsroom assistants or researchers before moving into a reporting role. With experience, they may go on to become senior broadcast journalists, become a studio-based presenter or correspondent. Those who start in radio would normally progress to posts with larger commercial or network stations, or move across into TV.

Finding vacancies

Most newspapers get plenty of applicants without needing to advertise, but many still advertise vacancies in their own appointments pages. Most nationally-advertised vacancies appear in *The Guardian* on Mondays and Saturdays (and online at www.guardian.co.uk/media), and the *Press Gazette* (online at www.pressgazette.co.uk). Details of vacancies and work experience placements within the BBC are available on their jobs site at www.bbc.co.uk/jobs – and those within ITV are available on their website at www.itvjobs.com.

Sources of further information

Broadcast Journalism Training Council – tel: 01778 440025. www.bjtc.org.uk

National Council for the Training of Journalists – tel: 01799 544014. www.nctj.com

Periodicals Training Council – tel: 020 7404 4168. www.ppa.co.uk

Skillset – the Sector Skills Council covering the advertsing industry. Helpline: 08080 300 900 (England and N. Ireland) or 0800 012 1815 (Wales). www.skillset.org/careers

Chapter nine

Careers using geography

This chapter focuses on the environment and land-based sector and also covers the following careers:

- cartographer

- environmental consultant

- land surveyor

- landscape architect

- town planner.

The chapter includes a career profile of a geography graduate working in an environmental role.

Current concern about climate change, shrinking energy resources and sustainability has put the environment at the heart of local, national and international affairs. But not only has the environment become a global political issue, it provides employment in safeguarding our environmental assets and securing a sustainable future. Tighter environmental legislation and the pressures of the green agenda have led to a growth in environmental careers. Lantra, the Sector Skills Council for environmental and land-based industries, has estimated that at least 46,000 new workers will be needed in the next ten years to meet the demands of this dynamic sector.

At present the environmental sector in the UK employs over 500,000 people in 17,000 companies and has an annual turnover of £25 billion. There are also 500,000 volunteer workers in environment and land-based organisations. The sector includes a range of environmental industries, from environmental management (pollution, climate change, sustainability management and recycling) to landscape (landscape architecture and garden design) and conservation (habitat management, countryside recreation, and the protection of rural and urban landscapes).

There are jobs within organisations such as local authorities, national parks, government agencies, countryside conservation organisations and water companies. The range of jobs in the sector is diverse, and the following are just some examples of jobs where your geography degree will be relevant.

Cartographer

As a cartographer your work would involve developing and producing maps, which could range from Ordnance Survey maps and road atlases to navigational charts and weather maps. You'd need a combination of scientific, technical and design skills to be able to represent natural features, such as landscapes, or distributions, such as population.

Traditional map-making methods have been replaced by the use of IT, enabling images to be generated and manipulated on screen. The development of geographical information systems (GIS) means that computerised maps can become part of sophisticated systems for seeing, modelling and analysing what is happening in the world.

Typically your work may involve:

- designing maps, graphics, illustrations and layouts

- using colour, symbols and styles to communicate information

- creating maps from aerial photographs

- remote sensing – using sensors in satellites and aircraft to gather spatial and environmental data about the earth

- working with GIS to see, model and analyse landscape features

- producing maps, both on screen and paper

- using desktop publishing packages to combine images and text ready for printing

- liaising with surveyors and designers.

You may be revising and updating existing maps or be working on regions that have not been mapped before. You could work for a national mapping agency, a government department or a commercial company. In a more senior role your work would involve managing projects, staff and resources.

Entry qualifications

You'll normally need a degree to become a cartographer. There are no specific degrees in cartography, but a range of degrees in relevant subjects including geography, surveying and mapping science, topographic science and geographical information systems. The British Cartographic Society (BCS) website (see below) lists undergraduate courses that include an element of cartography or a closely-related discipline such as spatial data visualisation and geo-visualisation.

You'll need to have design and IT skills, be able to interpret data and pay attention to detail, as well as a keen interest in geography and the environment.

Training and career development

Most large employers provide structured in-house training, focusing on developing practical cartographic skills, including the use of specific design software packages. On-the-job training may also be provided in areas such as digital mapping and GIS.

Postgraduate qualifications may be useful in terms of career development and it may be possible to seek sponsorship for study from your employer. There are several postgraduate courses in GIS or topographic sciences – again listed on the BCS website. The Royal Geographical Society offers chartered status with different routes for graduates and postgraduates.

Experience cartographers may progress to more senior or management roles. Government departments often have structured promotion routes, whereas in a small company you may need to be willing to relocate to progress in your career. Some cartographers choose to specialise in a particular area such as GIS.

Finding vacancies

Most cartographers are employed by commercial companies and you can find details of companies listed on the BCS website in the corporate members directory. You can find vacancies in the national press, on the websites of the BCS and the Society of Cartographers, in journals such as *Geomatics World*, and on websites such as Go-Geo! at www.gogeo.ac.uk which lists specialist recruitment agencies.

Sources of further information

Association for Geographic Information – tel: 020 7036 0430. www.agi.org.uk

British Cartographic Society – tel: 020 7591 3000. www.cartography.org.uk

Remote Sensing and Photogrammetry Society – tel: 011 5951 5435. www.rspsoc.org

Royal Geographical Society – tel: 020 7591 3000. www.rgs.org

Andrew Barker

Andrew describes his career progress within the Environment Agency and outlines his current responsibilities as a manager.

Career profile

Job title: area environment planning team leader

Employer: Environment Agency

Post-16 qualifications: A levels in geography, geology and film studies

Degree: BSc geography

Since finishing my geography degree I had some temporary jobs until I got a permanent job working for a local authority in the area of waste regulation and environmental protection. This position transferred to the Environment Agency on its formation.

When I was studying for my degree I decided that I wanted to work in the environment sector and also to work in a regulatory rather than commercial environment. I also wanted a job that offered challenges and development opportunities that would build on some of the skills I had developed while studying for my degree. I was also hoping for a career that would provide a working environment where there was a possibility to try new fields of work.

To this end I have held a number of positions in the Environment Agency including working in environment management, which involved regulating the waste industry, and working as a technical officer in the area of contaminated land and its associated clean up and redevelopment. I have also been involved in permitting waste sites to ensure that operations are conducted under tight environmental controls.

The Environment Agency has a duty to maintain and improve the quality of surface and ground waters and as part of the duty it monitors the quality of lakes, the sea and ground water on a regular basis. Our principal aims are to protect and improve the environment, and to promote sustainable development. To help deliver these aims I manage a team of environmental planners who are involved in the areas of water quality, water resource and waste management.

My responsibilities include managing and supporting the team so they can fulfil their roles and comply with the various internal management systems such as health and safety procedures. My duties also include budgetary control, acting as project executive for a number of environmental projects, recruitment, planning the work of the team and delivering the work in a manner that complies with the overall aims of the Environment Agency.

In my job you need to be able to negotiate and deal with a wide range of customers from a wide range of backgrounds. You also need an ability to interpret technical information and come to some decisions quickly about how to tackle an issue to achieve the best possible result for the environment. Other important skills are the ability to prioritise, communicate openly and honestly, and to be responsive to customer needs.

I enjoy managing my team of hardworking environmental planners, and I enjoy the fact that the work we do is helping to protect and improve the environment. I also like the conditions of employment and the opportunity to work with dedicated and professional colleagues.

The main challenges are that we have to manage our work to tight deadlines with limited resources, and so we need to work quickly and efficiently to ensure we comply with the requirements of the legislation we implement. Also the world is a constantly changing place, and we therefore need to remain constantly aware of new environmental threats. In terms of my future, I am committed to work in the area of environmental protection and improvement.

Environmental consultant

Environmental consultants are hired by commercial or government organisations to assist in a number of areas where environmental concerns and government legislation have to be adhered to. You could be brought in at the planning stage of a land development, or as part of an audit process, where a number of environmental assessments such as waste management and measuring contamination of land and water have to be made. Your tasks may involve data collection, auditing and analysis, and reporting results and findings.

Alternatively your work may involve considering the implications of new environmental legislation for your client, carrying out computer modelling to forecast environmental problems, or researching new ways to reduce environmental damage. Consultants work in a very commercial environment and senior staff may be employed to help attract future clients for the business or secure environmental sponsorship. You would either work for specialist consultancies with few staff, or for large, multidisciplinary consultancies.

Entry qualifications

You'll need at least a good honours degree to become an environmental consultant and most consultants have a scientific background. Relevant degrees include, for example, geography and environmental management as well are more science-based degrees such as geology, chemistry, geophysics and ecology management. It is a very competitive market and consultancies usually recruit graduates with a postgraduate qualification in a relevant subject or some work experience in that field. Work experience is also valuable and many employers offer placements linked to masters degrees. Some large consultancies, however, do offer graduate recruitment and training schemes.

You'll need to have a sound understanding of business practices, excellent communication skills, IT skills and an analytic approach to work. You'll also need good project management skills, as you'll probably be employed to assist or manage separate projects.

Training and career development

You will be encouraged to keep up to date with developments in the field and undertake short courses to gain specialist knowledge or a specialist qualification. Chartered institutions and professional bodies often provide training courses. Many universities also offer distance-learning courses that lead to higher qualifications. For future career development it is advisable to gain chartership via a professional body such as the Chartered Institution of Water and Environmental Management (CIWEM) or the Geological Society.

Typically your career will start in a junior position before progressing to senior consultant grade and ultimately principal consultant grade, where responsibilities are mainly team management, commercial development and being a technical specialist. Principal consultants often need to have professional membership of an appropriate body. It may be possible to progress further, to director level.

Finding vacancies

You can identify potential employers by researching companies in your area of interest, see ENDS directory (www.endsdirectory.com), and looking for graduate opportunities on their websites. You can also look for vacancies in the national and local press, specialist publications such as the *Environment Post* and *New Scientist*, and on recruitment sites such as stopdodo (www.eco-uk.com) and ENDS environmental job search (www.endsjobsearch.co.uk). Some vacancies are filled through personal contacts so it is important to build up and maintain contacts early in your career.

Sources of further information

Chartered Institution of Water and Environmental Management (CIWEM) – tel: 020 7831 3110. www.ciwem.org

Environmental Careers – www.environmentalcareers.org.uk

Geological Society – tel: 020 7434 9944. www.geolsoc.org.uk

Institute of Environmental Management and Assessment (IEMA) – tel: 01522 540069. www.iema.net

Institute of Ecology and Environmental Management (IEEM) – tel: 01962 868625. www.ieem.net

Land surveyor

Land (or geometrics) surveyors measure and collect data on specific areas of land. You could be assessing land due for redevelopment, or surveying a range of different areas such as landfill sites, pipeline and distribution systems, and airports.

Typically your work may involve:

- discussing project requirements with clients

- measuring the ground, including aspects such as angles and elevations

- gathering data on the Earth's physical and man-made features through surveys

- undertaking digital mapping

- using a range of equipment to produce surveys

- interpreting data using maps, charts and plans

- utilising data from a range of sources, such as aerial photography and satellite surveys

- using computer-aided design (CAD) and other IT software to interpret data and present information.

Architects, civil engineers, property developers, planners and cartographers all use the information that land surveyors produce. The work is an essential preliminary to planning, property development and construction, major engineering and other projects.

Traditional skills have largely been replaced by technological developments in mapping such as the global positioning system (GPS) and satellite imagery, which can accurately map anywhere in the world. Your skill as a surveyor would be in the management and use of this data.

Entry qualifications

Most entrants have a degree in surveying that has been accredited by a professional body such as the Royal Institution of Chartered Surveyors (RICS). With a relevant first degree such as geography, however, you can go on to take a RICS-accredited postgraduate degree. You can search for RICS-accredited courses on their website (see below).

As a land surveyor you'll be interpreting and analysing data, therefore you'll need to be observant and comfortable with numerical work. The work involves extensive use of computers so you would need to be confident in using the relevant software packages.

Training and career development

Due to rapid changes in technology land surveyors need to update their skills and knowledge on a regular basis. Training and continuing professional development also play a key role in gaining chartered status with the RICS, which can benefit career progression.

To become a chartered surveyor, you would need to complete two years of structured learning supported by RICS, while gaining practical work experience. This leads to a RICS professional assessment interview, known as the Assessment of Professional Competence (APC). After successfully completing the APC you can use the letters MRICS after your name.

As a land surveyor you could move into a range of sectors. The most common ones are construction, engineering and surveying, and you would normally start as a junior surveyor. With experience and training you can progress into a role as a surveyor, which in turn may lead on to more senior positions. There are opportunities to work abroad, or to branch out into areas such as archaeological surveying.

Finding vacancies

Directories of relevant employers are available from the Geomatics UK Network (www.geomatics.uk.net) and the RICS (at www.ricsfirms.com). Both the RICS and the Chartered Institution of Civil Engineering Surveyors (ICES) have links to job vacancies on their websites, and there are specialist recruitment sites such as www.earthworks-jobs.com and specialist agencies such as Macdonald and Company (www.macdonaldandcompany.com). Vacancies are also advertised in the press and industry magazines such as *Civil Engineering Surveyor* and *RICS Business*.

Sources of further information

Chartered Institution of Civil Engineering Surveyors (ICES) – tel: 0161 972 3100. www.ices.org.uk

Royal Institution of Chartered Surveyors (RICS) – tel: 0870 333 1600. www.rics.org

Landscape architect

Landscape architects specialise in planning, designing and managing open spaces, including both natural and built environments. They work on a diverse range of projects, from transforming derelict industrial sites to designing the layout of parks, gardens and housing estates. There is a huge increase in the need for good green spaces and landscape architects are at the forefront of developing sustainable communities and regenerating towns and cities.

Typically your work may involve:

- discussing landscape requirements with the client
- surveying the site and investigating its natural resources and features, as well as the plants and wildlife in the area
- consulting the local community about the proposed development
- preparing and presenting detailed plans using CAD packages
- choosing plants, shrubs and trees that will suit the land type and needs of the site
- estimating costs of construction and maintenance once it is complete
- submitting plans and estimates to the client
- visiting the site to make sure the designs are being followed and work is going smoothly.

You'd be involved in liaising closely with other professionals including architects, civil engineers, town planners, construction site supervisors and surveyors. Some landscape architects work alone, others in a team. Employers include the construction industry and public sector organisations, as well as private practice.

Entry qualifications

Most landscape architects have a degree or postgraduate qualification accredited by the Landscape Institute (LI). You'll need a degree to get a place on a postgraduate course, and geography is one of the subjects seen as being particularly useful. The LI website has a list of accredited courses offered by universities and colleges throughout the UK.

You'll need to have good design skills, excellent communication and negotiation skills, together with the ability to balance a number of demands and come up with a creative solution. You'll also need to have a genuine concern for the environment.

Training and career development

After successfully completing an accredited course you will be eligible for licentiate membership of the LI. To become a chartered landscape architect, members of the LI follow the Pathway to Chartership (P2C). Successful completion of the P2C leads to full membership of the LI and chartered status.

Training is ongoing and you will be expected to undertake continuing professional development throughout your career. Promotion prospects vary. In local government jobs there may be a defined promotion structure through to supervisory and management posts. Experienced practitioners often move into private practice, where they may be made a partner, or set up their own practice.

Finding vacancies

Vacancies are advertised on the websites of the LI and the Landscape Design Trust (see below), in specialist publications such as *Landscape Review*, and in local and national papers. There are also a number of specialist recruitment agencies, such as Hunter Dunning (www. hunterdunning.co.uk) You can also find a directory of landscape architect practices on the LI website.

Sources of further information

English Nature – tel: 0845 603 9953. www.englishnature.org

I want to be a landscape architect –
www.wanttobealandscapearchitect.com

Landscape Institute (LI) – tel: 020 7299 4500.
www.landscapeinstitute.org

Landscape Design Trust – tel: 01737 779257. www.landscape.co.uk

Lantra – tel: 0845 707 8007. www.lantra.co.uk and www.afuturein.com

Town planner

Town planners are involved in shaping the way our cities, towns and villages are built. They make short- and long-term decisions about the management and development of towns and the countryside. They have to strike a balance between the competing demands for land and its use, for example whether it should be developed for housing or parks. They present evidence and make recommendations to planning committees, government departments and developers on how land should be used.

Your work may involve a diverse range of activities, from visiting sites to assess the impact of proposed developments on people and the environment, to negotiating development proposals with local authorities and others. This would involve liaising with other professionals, such as architects and surveyors. When a developer gets planning permission, planners make sure the work meets the conditions laid down.

Around 50% of planners work for city, district and county councils. Other employers include government agencies and departments, planning consultancies, firms such as supermarket chains and property developers, and voluntary and environmental organisations.

Entry qualifications

You'll need a Royal Town Planning Institute (RTPI)-accredited qualification to work as a town planner. Royal Town Planning Institute-accredited first degrees in planning are available throughout the UK and last four years, or five years with a work placement. Graduates who haven't completed an RTPI-accredited planning course will need a recognised postgraduate qualification. If you have a first degree in a planning-related subject, such as geography, land surveying, landscape architecture, environmental science or geology, then you can go on to take an RTPI-accredited masters degree. A list of all accredited courses is available on the RTPI website.

You'll need to have excellent communication and negotiation skills, be able to carry out research and write reports, and work to deadlines. Most importantly you'll need to be able to take a balanced view and be aware of conflicting needs and interests.

Training and career development

After gaining an accredited qualification and at least two years of practical experience in planning you can apply to become a Chartered Town Planner and member of the RTPI (MRTPI). Members of the RTPI are expected to update their knowledge and skills through continuing professional development.

With chartered status and experience, planners may progress to senior planner posts. There are opportunities to move between the public sector and the private sector. It may be possible to specialise or to progress into a management position.

Finding vacancies

Vacancies are advertised on the website of the RTPI (see below), in local and national newspapers, on local government websites and on the local government job site (www.LGjobs.com), in *Planning Magazine* and on specialist websites (such as www.planningresource.co.uk). The RTPI website also has a link to an online directory of planning consultants.

Sources of further information

Commission for Architecture and the Built Environment – tel: 020 7070 6700. www.cabe.org.uk

Planning Resource – www.planningresource.co.uk

Royal Town Planning Institute (RTPI) – tel: 020 7929 9494. www.rtpi.org.uk

Chapter ten

Careers using history and archaeology

This chapter focuses on a number of career areas related to history and archaeology:

- archaeology work

- archivist

- museum and art gallery work – including education officer and curator

- heritage work – including heritage management and building conservation officer.

The chapter includes a career profile of an archaeology graduate working in the heritage sector.

Archaeology work

Archaeology is the study of our human past through physical remains. These range from buried cities to microscopic organisms. Archaeology, however, involves far more than digging up artefacts on historic sites. The work of the archaeologist may start with trying to locate a site, which may entail careful research, such as the study of aerial photographs and the use of remote sensing methods. Once digging starts, the position of every object found has to be precisely plotted in three dimensions. The position of an object, both on the site and in relation to other finds, often reveals more than the object itself.

Many delicate artefacts are preserved in the soil or under water, and start to decay as soon as they are exposed to the air. Conservation – preserving and caring for objects so that they survive after excavation – is a vital part of archaeological work. Finds have to be catalogued, photographed, drawn (drawings often reveal details not seen in photographs) and examined. Artefacts are studied, physically and chemically, to find out how they were made and to identify the origin of the raw materials. They also have to be dated, using a range of radiocarbon and other techniques. As you can see, archaeology spans the arts and sciences. Conservation and the examination of artefacts are usually carried out in laboratories by those who have studied science-based archaeology.

There are four main public archaeological bodies in the UK:

- English Heritage
- Historic Scotland
- Cadw (Welsh Historic Monuments)
- The Northern Ireland Environment Agency.

Each is responsible for the long-term conservation of ancient monuments and historic buildings, for promoting the public's understanding and enjoyment of our historic heritage, and for compiling and making available records of all the ancient monuments and sites in each country.

The National Trust, the National Trust for Scotland, the National Parks, local authorities and utility companies (such as water supply companies) employ archaeologists to record, survey and, occasionally, excavate sites in their care.

Many councils employ archaeologists. They advise on the recording and conservation of historic remains when planning applications are being considered, and ensure that fieldwork by independent bodies is carried out to a satisfactory standard.

Museums also offer a range of posts. Although there may be some fieldwork, keepers are more often responsible for the care or storage of artefacts, for research and for handling enquiries from the public, including identifying objects that people bring in. You might also find that curatorship is a suitable career – explored later in this chapter.

Entry qualifications

Although archaeology is an arts and humanities subject, it links with many disciplines including physics, chemistry, biology, geology, technology, the medical sciences, mathematics and geography as well as history, art, social science and religion. You can take either a BA or a BSc degree in archaeology, the BSc concentrating on archaeological science.

To work as a professional archaeologist, you'll normally need a degree in archaeology. The job market is highly competitive with many more graduates than vacancies. A postgraduate qualification may be helpful if a specialist skill, such as human bone analysis, is required.

It is immensely valuable to have experience of fieldwork (most degree courses include some field projects). Indeed, it's a good idea to join an archaeology society or the Young Archaeologists Club before you start your degree, and to take part in digs or other fieldwork.

To work on excavations, you need to be in good health, as working on digs in all weathers can be tough. Because you're trying to build up a picture of the past from many thousands of tiny bits of evidence, you must be patient and methodical. You should be a good team worker and have leadership potential. You'll have to collaborate with other disciplines, especially scientists, and you may have to supervise teams working on site. You'll also need to communicate clearly – orally and in writing; IT skills are also valuable.

Training and career development

Training tends to be through short, specialised courses that are relevant to the role. The Institute of Field Archaeologists (IFA) is the recognised professional institute. Membership is based on academic qualifications, experience and documented achievements. The IFA encourages continuing professional development (CPD) among its members.

Archaeologists tend to specialise in their work (over 80 specialisms have been identified). Archaeologists can specialise geographically, chronologically (such as prehistory, Roman, Anglo-Saxon, etc) or technically (such as site surveying, excavation, studying artefacts and so on).

Archaeology is a very small profession. Outside the national agencies (such as English Heritage), local authorities and universities, jobs tend to be short term and career prospects are limited. If you aim to be an excavation archaeologist, you will need to work your way up through the ranks – from excavator to site assistant to supervisor and so on. The main qualification for advancement is practical experience. In English Heritage you start as an assistant. Although much of the work is administrative, site experience is valuable if you are to progress to senior posts. Museums have their own career structure.

Finding vacancies

Many organisations advertise their vacancies through the British Archaeological Jobs and Resources (BAJR) website (www.bajr.org). The Institute of Field Archaeologists also runs a subscription Jobs Information Service (JIS). This produces a weekly bulletin and an online service that reproduces advertisements placed by employers and all the archaeological, heritage and research opportunities appearing in the national press and specialist journals during that week. See the website, at www.archaeologists.net.

You're also likely to find suitable jobs advertised in the national press and in *Museums Journal*.

Archaeology Abroad publishes a bulletin annually that provides information on hundreds of archaeological fieldwork opportunities outside the UK. See the website, at www.britarch.ac.uk/archabroad.

Sources of further information

Association of National Park Authorities – tel: 029 2049 9966. www.nationalparks.gov.uk

British Archaeological Job Resource – tel: 01620 861643. wwwbajr.org

Council for British Archaeology – tel: 01904 671417. www.britarch.ac.uk

English Heritage – tel: 0870 333 1181. www.english-heritage.org.uk

Forestry Commission – tel: 0131 334 0303. www.forestry.gov.uk

Institute of Field Archaeologists – tel: 0118 378 6446.
www.archaeologists.net

The National Trust – tel: 01793 817400. www.nationaltrust.org.uk

National Trust for Scotland – tel: 0844 493 2100. www.nts.org.uk

Archivist

Archivists preserve historical records. All sorts of organisations hold archives. They may include books, papers, maps, photographs, films and computer-generated records. Increasingly records are stored and preserved digitally. Archives are intended to be kept permanently, to preserve the past and allow others to discover it. Your work will include assisting people using the archives, promotional work including exhibitions, as well as the curatorial skills of selecting, arranging and cataloguing archives.

Most archivists work for central or local government. There are major archives of state and other papers held at the Public Records Office, split between sites in Kew and central London. Local archives are situated around the country. There are also limited openings in other organisations, including professional institutions, universities, hospitals, libraries, specialist museums, industry and research bodies.

Entry qualifications

You must have a good honours degree, a postgraduate qualification recognised by the Society of Archivists – courses currently offered are listed on their website (see below) – and a demonstrable interest in history. Many archivists have a degree in a historical field but it is not essential. Relevant work experience – paid or unpaid – is often required before you start postgraduate studies. Some institutions offer one-year paid graduate traineeships (see the Society of Archivists website, listed below).

You'll need to be able to undertake research, be comfortable with new technology, and be logical, as archives need identifying and sorting before they can be used. To help people conduct their research you must also be a skilled communicator; you must also be patient as they won't always know precisely what they're looking for!

Training and career development

Once qualified, archivists are encouraged to undertake the Society of Archivists Registration Scheme, which demonstrates a commitment to CPD and improves career chances. This is a very small profession and so opportunities for promotion to higher level posts may be limited. Progression may be from assistant archivist to senior posts with a more prominent management role. Some archivists move into records management. Opportunities for self-employed archivists are growing.

Finding vacancies

Vacancies are scarce in some parts of the country. You'll usually need to go wherever there is a vacancy – both for your first job and to develop your career. Vacancies are advertised on the Society of Archivists website (see below) and some are also advertised in the national press.

Sources of further information

Society of Archivists – tel: 01823 327030. www.archives.org.uk

Museum and art gallery work

The work of museums and art galleries is very similar and often overlaps. Museums collect, document, preserve, exhibit, interpret and store materials of historical, scientific and cultural interest. Art galleries do the same for paintings, sculpture and other works of art. Some institutions, such as the Victoria and Albert Museum in London, are both a museum and an art gallery.

Museums and art galleries increasingly are part of the leisure industry and aim to entertain as well as inform visitors. Because many aspects of the work are very similar, for the purpose of this chapter both types of institution are referred to as museums. There are four main types of museum:

- national
- university
- local authority
- independent.

The **national museums** include the British Museum, the National Gallery, the Natural History Museum, the Tate Galleries and the National

Museums of Scotland and Wales, as well as outstations (sites away from the main body of the museum) such as the Science Museum's National Railway Museum at York. These national museums provide about half of all museum jobs.

Most **university museums** are departmental collections used for teaching. These are staffed by university lecturers or laboratory technicians, who combine museum work with their other duties.

Local authority museums range from famous museums like the Museum of London, Manchester City Art Gallery and the Burrell Collection in Glasgow, through to small museums of local history with only one or two staff.

The largest growing group is the **independent museums**. These are funded by admission charges, grants, endowments and sponsorship. They have to be commercially successful, and so are run much more as businesses than other museums. They include sophisticated tourist attractions like the Jorvik Viking Centre in York, as well as hundreds of small special-interest ones.

Education officer

Many museums employ education staff. Education officers develop and deliver the museum's educational and learning programmes to primary and secondary schools. They may liaise with schools, organise visits, and teach classes in the museum and in schools. They also prepare teaching materials for school projects, hold workshops for teachers on how to make the best of the museum, run holiday events for young people and organise guided tours and talks.

Curator

The main concern of curators is to look after the museum's collections. You'd be responsible for acquiring objects and for researching, cataloguing, storing, displaying and explaining them. In the largest museums these would be your only duties and you might be able to specialise. But in most you'd be involved in all sorts of other jobs too, fundraising, answering visitor queries, security, setting up and publicising special exhibitions, giving talks and writing about the collection. In the smallest museums you might have to do all these things. Note that only the big national museums and the largest local authority museums offer positions where research is a major part of the job. As a curator in most museums you are not only responsible for the care of the collections, but must manage the museum or your department within it. This can include administration and managing staff.

Entry qualifications

To become an education officer, a teaching or community education background is usually required and your chances will be improved if you have successful teaching experience and an understanding of the National Curriculum. A postgraduate qualification in museum studies may also improve your employment opportunities. You need excellent written and oral communication skills, as well as teaching skills and team working skills.

To become a curator or art gallery keeper you'll normally need, in addition to a degree, a postgraduate qualification in museum studies. Competition for jobs is very fierce. The personal qualities required for curators differ somewhat between the types of museum. But there are some common aspects. You should be able to communicate your specialist knowledge clearly, lucidly and enthusiastically to non-specialists, be a good organiser, and have an empathy with your visitors and know what they want.

It is increasingly important for education officer and curator posts that you have prior work experience in the field as a volunteer. This will not only give you invaluable experience and a network of contacts, but will normally be expected by museum and art gallery recruiters. The Museums Association (MA) website at www.museumsassociation.org has information on organisations that run volunteer programmes. You could also approach local museums to enquire about volunteering.

Training and career development

If you are interested in museum work you should join the MA, which offers several CPD schemes for its members. The largest museums have well-established career structures and you can progress internally. Your career may lead from assistant curator/keeper through ranks of increasing seniority up to director with responsibility for running the whole museum. However, administration and management jobs are increasingly seen as distinct from that of curator, and the directors of some national museums have been appointed from outside the museum world. Elsewhere you are most likely to progress your career by moving between sectors, or progressing into consultancy work.

Finding vacancies

You can check for vacancies on the MA's website and in *Museums Journal* (published by the MA), but also look in the national press, and on the jobsite www.museumjobs.com. Check regional papers for jobs in local authority museums.

It may be worth looking at the opportunities with English Heritage (and its equivalents in Scotland, Wales and Northern Ireland), the National Trust and the National Trust for Scotland. These bodies preserve nationally-important monuments and historic buildings (and sometimes their contents). Although not museums, some of these organisations have openings for history graduates, for example, as education officers or site custodians.

Sources of further information

Associations of Independent Museums – tel: 02392 587751. www.aim-museums.co.uk

The Museums Association – tel: 020 7430 0730. www.museumsassociation.org

Museums, Libraries and Archives Council – tel: 0121 345 7300. www.mla.gov.uk

Heritage work

The heritage sector is a growing area of work and includes a number of different specialisms and opportunities concerned with the management, maintenance and conservation of historic sites, often combined with encouraging tourism. The range of sites includes:

- ancient monuments
- historic buildings, including industrial sites such as former collieries
- museums
- landscapes and gardens.

The largest employers are national organisations such as English Heritage and the National Trust. Other employers include the Churches of England, Wales and Scotland, local authorities, trusts, charities, privately-owned houses and societies such as the Victorian Society.

Ffion George

Ffion describes her route into the heritage sector, and outlines her current role as a custodian for the National Trust.

Career profile

Job title: custodian – Mr Hardman's Photographic Studio

Employer: National Trust

Post–16 qualifications: A levels in classical civilisation, English literature and philosophy

Degree: BA archaeology

Postgraduate qualification: MA museum and artefact studies

I always wanted to be an archaeologist when I was younger so it was a natural choice to study archaeology at degree level. Realistically, though, it's a very narrow field to get into and, while the degree gives you transferable skills, it doesn't prepare you for a career as such. During my degree I decided that a career with the National Trust was what I wanted. I've had a long-standing interest in the National Trust (my parents were members and I used to beg them for days out!) and it is closely related to archaeology. So I took an MA as a route into the museums and heritage sector.

I felt the MA would make me more employable as it had practical modules as well as theory. I was the sole project manager for an exhibition on Ancient Greece that was put up for three months and open to the public. I also had a four-week placement with the National Trust at their Dyrham Park property where I was assistant to the house and collections manager. Both were really good in terms of gaining experience.

I got a job more or less straight after the MA as a part-time house steward at Mr Hardman's Photographic Studio, but as soon as I arrived the custodian went on unexpected early maternity leave. I was then lucky enough to be offered the job as custodian to cover this leave. The experience on the MA of managing an exhibition, together with conservation experience during the MA and my degree, definitely helped in the interview.

As a custodian I am basically a housekeeper and the role is incredibly varied, from beating carpets (we're cleaning the whole house at the moment in preparation for opening for the season) to organising for an electrician to fix a light. I am responsible for managing the house, the house steward and the team of volunteers. I've recently designed an exhibition for the property called Cameras and Camisoles, focusing on the life and achievement of Mr Hardman's wife. We have objects on display and the volunteers are going to tell the story during a guided tour.

You need to be very adaptable in this job. Self-motivation and self-management are also essential, as is conservation knowledge – you need to know how to handle delicate objects. People skills are really important as I have a lot of volunteers to manage. I really enjoy the variety of the job, and the staff and volunteers are fantastic, so it's a good environment to work in. I really love working with the volunteers. They are doing it because they love it and so am I – so we all have a common interest. It is also a challenge to manage the volunteers, as you have to be respectful and tactful towards them as they are giving up their free time.

My aim for the future is to carry on working for the National Trust and work my way up the career ladder. I'd like to become the property manager of one of their estates.

Heritage manager

Heritage managers at any site need to balance the needs of visitors and tourists, landowners and farmers, and archaeologists and historians. Your work activities will vary depending on the specific function of the post and the setting in which it takes place. In larger attractions, responsibility for managing the property, the collections and visitor services are likely to be shared between a number of managers. At smaller sites you may be responsible for all of these activities.

Typically your work may involve:

- organising and monitoring conservation and maintenance of the site

- planning the development of the site and deciding on special events/exhibitions

- generating income from commercial activities such as catering, entrance fees and membership schemes
- promoting the attraction through publicity, public relations and marketing activities
- recruiting, supervising and monitoring staff and volunteers
- managing budgets
- overseeing the day-to-day operations, including catering facilities and car parking.

You'd be involved in liaising with external agencies such as funding bodies, professional associations and tourist bodies. You'd also need to keep up to date with developments in the field and with historical research into topics related to the attraction.

Entry qualifications

Entrants usually have a degree in subjects such as history or history of art, archaeology, heritage or museum studies, marketing or other business-related subjects, geography or countryside management. Many entrants hold relevant postgraduate qualifications in heritage/ museum management. A lot of postgraduate courses also include a work placement or work-based project.

Getting some seasonal work as a tour guide, interpreter or in visitor reception is a good way to gain initial work experience. Voluntary experience is extremely valuable too and heritage sites offer opportunities to volunteer in a variety of roles. As a volunteer on English Heritage's Education Volunteering Programme (available at ten of its sites), for example, you would be assisting with site-based education activities. As a volunteer with the National Trust you may work directly with the public or on practical conservation projects.

You'll need to have the ability to deal effectively with a wide range of people, commercial awareness and customer service skills, and a genuine interest in and understanding of the heritage sector.

Training and career development

The large national bodies and local authorities run in-house training courses, for example in management skills and heritage issues. The Association for Heritage Interpretation (AHI) runs short courses. The MA also runs courses and CPD events.

If you don't already have a postgraduate qualification you may be encouraged to take a part-time masters in heritage management or museum studies while working.

You may choose to move between areas within heritage management, such as events management, visitor services or education. Gaining a range of skills in managing people, budgets and projects will help your career development. If you're looking to progress into senior management then you will need substantial business and financial experience.

Finding vacancies

You can check for vacancies on the MA's website, in *Museums Journal*, on the websites of national organisations, in the national press and on the jobsite www.museumjobs.com. Check regional papers for seasonal and entry-level posts.

Sources of further information

Association for Heritage Interpretation – tel: 0560 274 7737. www.ahi.org.uk

Association of National Park Authorities – tel: 029 2049 9966. www.nationalparks.gov.uk

English Heritage – tel: 0870 333 1181. www.english-heritage.org.uk

The National Trust – tel: 01793 817400. www.nationaltrust.org.uk

Building conservation officer

Building conservation officers help to protect and enhance historic buildings such as houses, lighthouses, windmills, churches and factories. They aim to secure the improvement of historic places for the benefit of communities now and in the future. They may work within communities, encouraging them to support their historic places. They also advise property owners on alterations or improvements to buildings, and encourage them to preserve the character of historic properties.

Typically your work may involve:

- inspecting and surveying historic buildings and writing reports on their condition

- recommending buildings for conservation and producing a schedule of work required

- finding suppliers and craftspeople who can provide the traditional skills to carry out the work

- estimating conservation and restoration costs

- making sure that the work complies with legislation

- giving advice on building conservation to owners, architects, heritage groups and other bodies

- working alongside conservation and heritage groups, and government agencies, to develop policies on building conservation.

Entry qualifications

You'll normally need a degree to become a building conservation officer. A small number of universities offer specific degrees in architecture conservation or building conservation. Other relevant degrees include planning, building/construction, civil/structural engineering, surveying, architecture, history with an architecture component and archaeology. Many entrants also have a relevant postgraduate qualification. The Institute of Historic Building Conservation (IHBC) is the professional body for building conservation practitioners and you can find a list of IHBC-approved courses on its website (see below).

This is a very small and competitive field. Many employers look for people with experience so getting some voluntary work experience with a conservation organisation would be advisable. This could be with English Heritage, the National Trust or with one of the national amenity societies – you can find a list of these societies on the website of the Joint Committee of the National Amenity Societies at www.jcnas.org.uk.

You'll need to have excellent negotiating and communication skills, an eye for architectural detail, and a strong interest in historic architecture and building methods.

Training and career development

Training is mainly on the job, and through attending training events run by specialist bodies such as the IHBC and the Society for the Protection of Ancient Buildings (SPAB). As a building conservation specialist you may also work towards relevant NVQs including:

- NVQ level 4 in building site management (conservation)

- NVQ level 4 in conservation control

- NVQ level 5 in conservation consultancy.

Typically your career may start with a trainee position at conservation officer level in a local authority. You may be promoted to senior or management roles. You may choose to move between organisations and take on specialist roles. With substantial experience and industry contacts you may decide to become a consultant, focusing on advisory and design work.

Finding vacancies

You can check for vacancies in local and national newspapers, on the website of the IHBC, on the websites of national organisations and on specialist recruitment websites. You can also search for live vacancies in local councils at www.LGtalent.com.

Sources of further information

Ancient Monuments Society – tel: 020 7236 3934. www.ancientmonumentssociety.org.uk

English Heritage – tel: 0870 333 1181. www.english-heritage.org.uk

The Georgian Group – tel: 087 1750 2936. www.georgiangroup.org.uk

Institute of Historic Building Conservation – tel: 01747 873133. www.ihbc.org.uk

The National Trust – tel: 01793 817400. www.nationaltrust.org.uk

The Society for the Protection of Ancient Buildings – tel: 0207 377 1644. www.spab.org.uk

The Victorian Society – tel: 0208 994 1019. www.victoriansociety.org.uk

Chapter eleven

Careers using languages and linguistics

This chapter covers the following career areas:

- interpreting and translating
- linguistics work – speech and language therapy
- teaching English as a foreign language (TEFL).

The chapter includes a career profile of a languages graduate working as a translator.

Interpreting and translating

Interpreting

There are two forms of interpretation – consecutive and simultaneous. In the first you listen to a speech, either in part or whole, and then relay it to the audience. This may mean taking notes as reminders of what was said. This method is slow, because the audience must listen to the original then the translation (or even translations!).

Simultaneous interpretation involves translating what you hear immediately to your audience as the speaker continues to talk. You may do this on a one-to-one basis, known as whispering – because you whisper your interpretation into your client's ear. More often simultaneous work involves sitting in a soundproof booth and listening to the speaker through headphones. You speak your interpretation into a microphone that feeds your voice to the headphones of your audience.

Simultaneous interpretation is generally accepted as the more stressful work, because there is almost no thinking time. To ease the pressure, two interpreters often work together, alternating in sessions lasting perhaps half an hour. But this isn't always the case. Interpreters can sometimes work for three hours or more without a break.

In either form of interpretation, you must have an excellent knowledge of both languages. There are many words and sayings in any language that can't be translated directly into another, so you must be able to give far more than just a literal translation. The only full-time work for interpreters is in conference interpreting, and this is a tiny profession. Conference interpreters always work from the foreign language into their own language.

Most conference interpreters work for international bodies such as the United Nations (UN) and its many agencies, the institutions of the European Union (EU), NATO, and so on. As an interpreter you may have to travel worldwide to translate at the conferences and meetings attended by representatives of such bodies. There are also self-employed interpreters and those employed by specialist communications agencies. Both tend to do other interpreting and translation work in addition to conference work. They too are expected to travel in pursuit of their work.

Businesses also need interpreters, for example during trade fairs, when receiving delegations from abroad and in negotiating overseas contracts. In this case you will translate both ways – into and out of your own language. This is usually part-time self-employed work, although some companies are large enough to require full-time interpreters.

If you can speak a language used by UK immigrants and refugees – such as Pashto (from Afghanistan), Hindi (India), Urdu (Pakistan) and Albanian – you may find work (usually self-employed or part time) in public service interpreting helping local authority departments, the courts, medical staff and the police.

Translating

To be a good translator, it is not enough to have a good knowledge of languages. You must be able to translate idiomatically and to write lucidly and succinctly. Translators work into their own language. The work is usually of two types – literary, or technical and commercial.

Literary translation covers novels, poetry, plays, biographies and similar material. Almost all translators in this field are self-employed and few can make a living this way. The work is generally very difficult, because you must catch the 'spirit' not just the literal meaning of the work. You are producing a paraphrase rather than a translation.

Technical and commercial translation is more straightforward and offers the best work prospects. Accuracy is the most important aspect of this work. Work can range from translations of books, through scientific papers and legal documents, to technical manuals. Translators may do a lot of internet research as well as using dictionaries and other reference books. It helps to have an in-depth knowledge of the specialist subject and its terminology, as well as the language.

Most of the work is done on a freelance basis, although some translators are full-time employees. Most of the latter work for international bodies such as the UN and EU, and for larger government departments and the Government Communications Headquarters (GCHQ), translation agencies and large multinational companies.

Entry qualifications

You will need fluency in two or more languages. Most entrants to translation and interpreting have a degree, normally in modern language subjects, languages combined with another subject, or in translation. For interpreter posts a postgraduate qualification, such as a masters degree in interpreting techniques, is also usually expected. For translator posts, though not essential, a postgraduate degree such as a masters degree in translation will definitely increase your job prospects. It can also be an advantage to show first-hand experience of another language through having lived and worked abroad.

For translator and interpreter posts each organisation has its own entry requirements. For staff translator posts in the EU and UN, for example, you must pass written and oral entrance exams. For staff interpreter posts in the EU and UN you will need to have a masters degree from an establishment recognised by the Directorate General for Interpretation.

Training and career development

The Institute of Translation and Interpreting (ITI) offers short courses and workshops, and different levels of membership for interpreters and translators – qualified membership being a mark of professional recognition.

Most interpreters start in other careers where they can use their languages and do freelance interpreting on the side. As their skills improve, they may continue to work as a freelance or they may try to enter one of the organisations recruiting full-time staff. With experience, conference interpreters may become consultant interpreters, recruiting teams of interpreters for private employers.

Most translators work freelance. Many start out as an in-house translator, for a translation agency or company, and then move into freelance work. Translators who are employed by international bodies such as the EU have a good chance of being promoted as there is a clear career grading scheme. It may be possible to specialise in one area of translating, such as law, medicine, science or engineering.

For freelance translators and interpreters, progression depends on building experience, reputation and contacts. With experience, some freelancers set up their own translation agency. Although there is no formal career development, earnings for the successful can be relatively high. However, for most people in translation and interpreting work, the life is an uncertain one.

Finding vacancies

Most permanent posts are advertised in the national press or on the internet. Your best chance for freelance work is to register with an agency. If you want to work in conference interpreting, you should become a member of AIIC, which is the professional body for the industry. Most organisations prefer to use AIIC interpreters because they will be assured of their professional capability; AIIC is an international organisation with members in over 65 countries.

Sources of further information

AIIC – tel: 0041 22 908 1540. www.aiic.net

CILT: The National Centre for Languages – tel: 020 7379 5101. www.cilt.org.uk

Chartered Institute of Linguists – tel: 020 7940 3100. www.iol.org.uk

Institute of Translation and Interpreting – tel: 01908 325250. www.iti.org.uk

National Register of Public Service Interpreters – tel: 020 7940 3166. www.nrpsi.co.uk

Andrew Leigh

Andrew, a self-employed translator, describes how he has chosen to use languages throughout his career, and outlines his current responsibilities as a freelancer.

Career profile

Job title: translator

Post-16 qualifications: A levels in French, Spanish, history and general studies

Degree: BA modern languages (studying French and Spanish)

Postgraduate qualifications: PGCE (Postgraduate Certificate in Education) and MA translation

After my degree I took a PGCE and went on to teach in a secondary school for two years. I'd always wanted to use my languages for a specific purpose, which I was doing, but I missed using languages at a higher level and missed the intellectual challenge.

I wanted to spend some time abroad so I took a TEFL (Teaching English as a foreign language) course and taught in Spain for a year. When I came back I took a masters degree in translation. I'd really enjoyed doing translation during my degree and my main motivation was to carry on using my languages. During the course I learned Italian and Portuguese, and the practical skills to become a proper translator.

I then got a job as an in-house translator with an agency in London translating a variety of legal, financial, business and commercial documents. After three years I decided on a lifestyle change, moved to Sheffield and became a freelance translator. I am also now a Qualified Member of the Institute of Translation and Interpreting.

I work for a number of agencies, mainly translating French, Spanish and Italian documents into English. As part of my degree course I spent some time in France (working) and Spain (as a student), which has come in useful. The work involves a lot of internet research to find the right terminology to use. For example, there might be ten possible translations for one word! A lot of the work I do is legal translation and I have to be very accurate, using the correct legal terminology. It helps to have a background to the case to put the document in context, which can also involve internet research.

To be a translator you need the ability to write well, good research skills, a good eye for detail, and to be meticulous and patient. As a freelancer you also need excellent time management skills to meet deadlines, and to be able to manage yourself in terms of finances and so on.

I really like the intellectual challenge of translating and to me translating a document is a pleasurable thing. I also like being self-employed, as there's no commuting, no boss and no office politics! The downside to freelancing is that you generally work on your own and the workflow can be unpredictable, although I am usually busy all the time. There is also no defined career progression.

With this in mind I started studying part time for a law degree and am now in my third year. I had a dual aim. Firstly, to be able to understand legal areas a lot better, to help in the translation of legal documents and, secondly, so I can really market myself as a legal translator. There is a gap in the market for this kind of specialist and in the short term my aim is to set up my own legal translation business and build up my client base. Ultimately, in the longer term I'd like to have my own agency and be in the position to take on other people.

Linguistics work

Linguistics is the scientific study of language. It involves the study of sounds and how they are made, grammatical constructions and how meaning is conveyed. You may study linguistics as a subject in its own right, or as a specialist paper forming part of a modern languages degree. There are few occupations where you can use the subject directly, although linguistic theories are applied in various careers including teaching, social work and computing. For example, the computing industry aims to produce programs that will translate from one language to another. This calls for people who can analyse the structure of languages and design appropriate software. However, the career that will probably make most direct use of your specialist knowledge is speech and language therapy.

Speech and language therapy

Speech therapists assess and treat speech, language and voice defects of all kinds. The National Health Service (NHS) employs the vast majority. They work in clinics, hospitals, special schools and patients' homes. Those working in rural areas may have a lot of travelling to do.

People are referred to speech therapists by their teachers, doctors or hospital consultants for a range of problems. A lot of the patients are children. They may be very slow in learning to talk, find it difficult to articulate, or have a stammer or hearing difficulties. They may have physical disabilities or learning difficulties. Working with adults may involve helping people who have lost the ability to speak through illness or accident. Someone whose brain has been damaged through an accident or stroke may have to relearn how to speak and use language. People who have had their larynx (voice box) removed need to develop an alternative method of sound production. Although some people are treated in groups, most get individual treatment. Therapists also attend case conferences and must work closely with doctors, social workers, psychologists, teachers and other professionals.

You'll need to understand people of all ages and temperaments and be able to win their confidence. You must communicate clearly. You need to be patient because treatment can often be long and difficult. You will also need to be well organised because your work is largely unsupervised and you have to arrange your own schedules.

Entry qualifications

To become a speech and language therapist you would need to have a recognised first degree or postgraduate qualification in speech and language therapy and to be registered with the Health Professions Council (HPC). Degree courses last three or four years and are listed in the *My Career in Speech and Language Therapy* careers guide published by the Royal College of Speech and Language Therapists (RCSLT) (available to download at www.rcslt.org). Some courses require specific GCSEs and A levels, such as English and biology, so check individual entry requirements. If you have a degree in a related subject, such as linguistics or psychology, you must take a two-year postgraduate qualifying course.

Training and career development

Newly-qualified speech and language therapists complete a programme including regular clinical supervision and specialist advice, and can go on to access a wide range of post-registration education and training opportunities. There are opportunities to work in the NHS, education or private sector. You may be able to progress into areas of clinical specialism, research or management. In the NHS, there is a promotion ladder.

Finding vacancies

Vacancies are advertised in the RCSLT's fortnightly *Bulletin Supplement*. The *Bulletin* can also be viewed online by registered members of the RCSLT at the website listed below. NHS jobs are advertised at www.jobs.nhs.uk.

Sources of further information

Health Professions Council – tel: 020 7840 9802. www.hpc-uk.org

Royal College of Speech and Language Therapists – tel: 020 7378 1200. www.rcslt.org

Teaching English as a foreign language (TEFL)

Teaching English as a foreign language (TEFL) involves teaching English to students whose first or main language is not English. Your students may be taught abroad or in the UK. They may be students wanting to study at a British university, or business people who need to learn English, or people wanting to improve their conversational English.

Most openings for TEFL are overseas, mainly in Western Europe and the Middle East, with commercial language schools, voluntary organisations, large employers and the British Council. Overseas contracts are often for a fixed term. There are also opportunities in the UK, particularly in commercial language schools.

As part of a languages degree you might spend a period of time working abroad as an assistant, teaching English to secondary school students. This would give you a flavour of teaching work, and also allow you to learn something of the culture of the host country.

Teaching English to speakers of other languages (TESOL) is often used to mean the same thing as TEFL, but it is also used to describe English language teaching to people living in an English-speaking country who are not native English speakers, such as refugees or first-generation immigrants. For more information on TESOL, which TEFL also comes under the umbrella of and shares the same entry qualifications, please refer to Chapter thirteen.

Chapter twelve

Careers using music, drama and dance

This chapter focuses on performance work and other career options, and covers the following areas:

- music performance – classical and popular
- music therapy
- drama – acting in theatre, radio, television, film, commercials
- dance
- stage management.

Where appropriate, information has been included on alternative training for performers, so that you can see whether or not a degree will be the best route for you to follow. The chapter includes a career profile of a classical singer.

Many people are attracted to the idea of working in the performing arts, for example as an actor, dancer or musician. Performing arts, however, is a very competitive industry. There are few permanent posts and many performers have to supplement their income through temporary or other part-time work. Therefore if you want to become a performer it would be useful to get some work experience to give you some transferable or key work skills.

Nearly all professional performers have had training at either a drama or dance school or at university. When considering careers using music, drama or dance, you need to be aware of the limitations of some of the degrees in these fields. University degree courses in these subjects may include a large element of performance, but they are not usually intended as a substitute for the kind of performance courses (including degree courses) offered by the specialist music, drama and dance academies, which are more vocational and practical.

However, a university degree can equip you for careers in production, stage management, direction, arts administration (see Chapter fifteen for further information on arts administration) and management. You can also teach music, drama or dance in primary and secondary schools if you obtain a postgraduate teaching qualification.

To be a professional actor, stage singer or dancer it's vital to have an Equity card. This is the membership card of the British Actors Equity Association – the trade union of the profession. It allows you to apply for vacancies advertised as Equity only. Equity will only issue a membership card once you have produced a required number of professional contracts, unless you have graduated from an accredited course.

If you join a full-time higher education course lasting a year or more that prepares you for a career as an actor (or as a theatre director, dancer, choreographer, singer or for a related career), you can become a student member (£15 to join, including the first year's subscription). This offers a number of benefits.

You can get full Equity membership on graduation without having to provide proof of work if you are:

- on a course accredited by the National Council of Drama Training (NCDT) or the Council for Dance Education and Training (CDET)

- studying theatre design

- studying singing at a conservatoire

- on the musical theatre course at the Royal Academy of Music.

If you are on a non-accredited course then you can continue at the student rate for up to two years, which allows time for you to get professional employment and become eligible for full membership.

Music performance

Performance work can be divided into two categories, classical and popular music, although there is a good deal of overlap between the two.

Classical musicians play in orchestras, ensembles or chamber groups. A minority also work as soloists. Some symphony orchestras, opera houses and smaller groups employ musicians on a full-time salaried basis. Others use freelance players who also play for other groups. Singers, similarly, may be salaried members of a professional choir, but most work freelance. There are opportunities in opera, oratorio, solo recitals and various types of concert work, which include light music and cabaret.

Popular music ranges from pop and rock, through country and western and folk, to jazz, dance music and musicals. Some popular musicians combine playing an instrument, often a synthesiser or guitar, with singing. Many popular musicians compose, write and perform their own material, and spend periods of time recording songs in recording studios.

Many freelance musicians work as session musicians, recording music for films, radio and television programmes, commercials and jingles, and backing tracks for singles and albums. Many also supplement their income by part-time private teaching.

Classical musicians and popular musicians spend their time rehearsing, performing and practising. Hours can be long and unsociable. Most performances are given in the evenings and at weekends. Musicians also travel a lot, either to performances or while on tour in Britain or abroad.

Entry qualifications

Many musicians have a degree or other qualification in music. To enter a music degree course you'll normally need two or three A levels or the equivalent, including music, plus an audition. These courses vary a lot in content and emphasis so you'll need to research them carefully. There are two types of undergraduate degrees in music, the BA (Bachelor of Arts) and the BMus (Bachelor of Music).

The BA teaches a broad musical education and the chance to study academic subjects, whereas the BMus is performance focused and more likely to be offered by music conservatoires. Conservatoires are specialist music training colleges. They are designed to prepare talented musicians for careers as performers, so if you have your heart set on performing they are probably the best option as they offer an opportunity to specialise early on. University graduates with a good first degree in music can opt to go on to take a postgraduate performance course at a conservatoire. Students with degrees from conservatoires also usually go on to take postgraduate study.

If you want to be a musician you'll need to have outstanding musical ability, a wide repertoire of music, and be self-disciplined and dedicated. You'll need to take any opportunity that arises, for example through student music groups, amateur orchestras, festivals and auditions, to gain experience and build your contacts.

Training and career development

Many musicians continue to pay for their own lessons to further develop their music skills. Continuous improvement is fundamental to the art of a performer, and if you aspire to becoming a concert soloist, you'll continue to undertake tuition throughout your working life.

Classical musicians can develop successful careers through playing in orchestras, small ensembles, professional choruses, conducting, composing and working in music education. Very few earn their living as solo performers, and those who do progress to become soloists are likely to have started by combining freelance solo work with teaching.

Apart from musicians in orchestras (where they can move up the ladder to senior posts) there is no career progression path for most professional musicians. Most musicians aspire to having regular work, being able to work full time as a musician, and to be able to work with other musicians they admire.

Finding vacancies

Most professional musicians are self-employed, although there are some opportunities on cruise ships, in holiday camps and theatre companies. Networking and personal contacts are very important and often a common way of finding work in the music field, as vacancies are often filled by word of mouth.

Jenny Rust

Jenny describes the route she has taken to become a classical singer, the skills you need to be a good performer and the current work she is involved in.

Career profile

Job title: classical singer

Post-16 qualifications: A levels in music, theatre studies and business studies

Degree: BA music

Postgraduate qualification: Postgraduate Diploma (PGDip) in vocal performance

I chose my degree because I wanted to pursue my interest in music. I took a classical performance module with singing as my instrument and really enjoyed it. I also met a singing teacher who really opened up my voice and encouraged me to go further with it. So by my third year I had decided this was the career I wanted to follow, and sang in some choirs and arranged and performed recitals to get some experience.

A voice takes time to mature and the best time to start classical singing is in your mid-twenties, so I took some time out before applying for postgraduate training. During this time I got some experience in amateur opera. I also did some administration work. As opera is such an unreliable industry this means I will always have temping to fall back on. It also helped to fund my next course!

I then took a Postgraduate Diploma in vocal performance at the Royal Scottish Academy of Music and Drama in Glasgow (RSAMD). I'm currently taking a continuing education course at the RSAMD, which includes singing lessons, vocal performance and languages. I'm funding my course by working part time in a supermarket and teaching singing lessons. Next year I shall be going on to take a masters degree in vocal performance at the Royal Northern College in Manchester.

To be a classical singer you obviously need a good voice! I've always enjoyed singing and when I was at school I was in a choir and various theatre groups. You need to have music theory under your belt – preferably to at least grade 5. I would also advise anyone to get good piano skills so they can supplement their income by teaching. You also need to learn the languages for opera – Italian, German and French.

To be a good performer you need enthusiasm and stamina. You also need to keep positive and self-motivated. This is one of the main challenges. I have to sit and practise for around two hours every day, learning the notes and practising the technique in the songs I'm working on. I also have to work on memorising a piece in the language it's written in. You have to be prepared to audition for everything too, which can be daunting, and to receive criticism and rejection, so you need to have confidence in yourself.

What I enjoy about singing and performing is putting everything together that you have been working on for a long time, to make it look easy! I enjoy performing in a production, when a story comes to life and all the emotion of the music is shown in every character.

I've had a role as Pamina in The Magic Flute and some chorus roles in amateur opera.

I've also been in the City of Birmingham Symphony Orchestra (CBSO) Chorus, which sings at major events. All big orchestras have choruses. It's not paid work, but very high-level amateur, and another way of getting good experience.

I'm currently organising and performing concerts with a group of singers. I also do solos for local choral societies and sing at weddings. It's very much about developing contacts in this line of work, and now I'm getting known the offers are coming in. So I'm actually earning money from singing!

In the future I will start auditioning for opera choruses to get experience of the opera stage, and then start auditioning for solo roles with opera companies. My ultimate ambition is to sing lead soprano roles in an international opera house such as Covent Garden!

Music therapy

Music therapists use the effects of music to help people with a wide range of problems, including people with physical or learning difficulties, mental health problems and stress-related illnesses. This has led to the appointment of music therapists working in education, health and social services. The acts of making and listening to music can help people to relax, provide them with mental stimulus and give them an emotional outlet.

Entry qualifications

Music therapy is a state registered profession. To use the title music therapist, you must complete at least three years of full-time musical education and then take a postgraduate masters degree recognised by the Association of Professional Music Therapists (APMT) and approved by the Health Professions Council (HPC), and then register with the HPC.

You'll need to have a high level of musicianship combined with excellent communication skills and an open, non-judgmental outlook.

Training and career development

A large part of the training involves practical clinical placements under the direct supervision of a qualified music therapist. Placements take place in schools, hospitals and other centres. Once registered as a music therapist, you will need to undertake continuing professional development (CPD) throughout your career.

Music therapists may move into management, research or training roles. With experience and contacts they may go on to set up their own private music therapy practice.

Finding vacancies

The APMT advertises vacancies on the members section of its website, and jobs in the National Health Service (NHS) are advertised on www.jobs.nhs.uk.

Drama

There are five main areas of employment for actors:

- theatre
- radio
- television
- film
- commercials.

There are two main areas of theatre employment – touring companies and theatre companies. At one time almost every town had its own repertory theatre. These were the main learning grounds for novice actors. Today these have largely been replaced by touring companies. These perform for a few days at a time in a theatre, hall or other venue and then move on to the next. Actors may perform several plays during a tour.

Theatre companies are usually set up for one particular play or show. Shows normally run for a fixed number of weeks or months. If the show is particularly successful, the run may be extended or the show may be transferred to another theatre. If the show fails, it closes early. Some actors specialise in pantomime and summer shows.

Radio uses actors in plays, poetry readings, soaps, dramatised features, serial readings, comedy and other programmes. Most work, apart from soaps and serials, is on a one-off basis. Unlike theatre, you don't have to learn your lines but work from a script instead. On the other hand, you have only your voice with which to create characters.

Actors are usually employed to work on one-off programmes, although there are opportunities in series of various lengths. Television work can be difficult to enter until you have repertory or similar broad experience. It can also be difficult competing for a part against a well-known actor.

Television directors, like film directors, record programmes in a series of short takes. These rarely last more than a minute or two. Actors usually learn their lines beforehand, then rehearse each take on the set and then record it at once. Scenes are often shot out of sequence. It needs skill and self-discipline on the part of the actors if characters are to develop through a story. There is also a lot of waiting time on set while equipment is prepared and technical problems are sorted out, so you must be patient. Although it's harder to develop a character than it is on the stage, the work is generally better paid and introduces the actor to a vastly bigger audience.

The film industry is small and opportunities are limited. Although it can take months to produce a film, most actors are hired for a few days or weeks. Extras don't need to be Equity members unless they have a speaking part. The techniques used in filming are similar to those used in television, although locations are often more exotic and the pay is better. You must be prepared to work outside the UK.

Commercials can be a useful way to boost your income, but should not be seen as a way into other areas of acting. Moreover, the work is rarely regular. Work always comes through casting agencies. Television commercials are well paid, radio less so. If you're in a fairly high-profile television campaign, you mustn't accept work for a competing product. If you do, you're likely to lose the chance to do any future commercial work.

Entry qualifications

Nearly all professional actors have trained, often in specialist drama schools. The National Council for Drama Training (NCDT) recommends all intending actors to complete a course of recognised training. Details of full-time courses at the 22 schools that are members of the Conference of Drama Schools (CDS) are listed in *The CDS Guide to Careers Backstage*, which is available as an ebook that you can download as a pdf at www.drama.ac.uk. There is a variety of courses on offer, including three-year degrees in professional acting.

Once you graduate from a course accredited by the NCDT, you qualify for an immediate Equity card. Contracts are difficult to obtain without an Equity card. Graduates can sometimes get into fringe and alternative theatre and then build up enough experience to apply for an Equity card.

Accredited drama schools usually only accept students over the age of 18. They offer tailored, vocational courses that are recognised by the industry, and which have strong links with agents, casting directors, production companies and broadcasters. It is not easy to get into an accredited drama school. Your potential is assessed by interview and audition.

There are university degree courses in drama, but some are more academic than performance based, so you should check the course content. As a graduate you could choose to go on to take a postgraduate course at a drama school.

Training and career development

Actors don't tend to have a specific career route and come from a variety of backgrounds. Some start their careers in theatre, often working initially in stage management and progressing to acting roles on stage. Others may be successful in auditioning for television commercials, radio or television drama series, or film roles, and build up their reputation this way.

Actors develop their skills on the job, through rehearsal and performance, and gaining experience. They may choose to take further classes in voice and music training. Some actors choose to undertake further training and qualifications to move into related fields such as scriptwriting, teaching, directing or drama therapy.

Finding vacancies

Most acting jobs are short term and many actors have to take other work to supplement their income. Competition is fierce and you'll need to promote yourself through registering with casting directories such as Spotlight at www.spotlight.com. Equity's website has a job information section for its members. Most professional actors are represented by an agent.

Dance

Dancers use performance to bring a story to life. As a dancer you will be expected to perform either for live audiences or for recorded media, including film, television and music videos. A choreographer, producer or director will cast you for a role. For roles in musical productions, dancers increasingly need to be able to sing.

Dancers must be able to work in a variety of styles including, for example:

- jazz
- tap
- ballet
- modern
- ballroom
- flamenco
- country.

The more styles you can work in, the more likely you are to find work. You will work closely with choreographers and other dancers to realise the producer's or director's vision. To create an effective production you will need to train, rehearse and work with other dancers in a collaborative effort.

Working days on film or television sets can be very long, so you will need to be able to manage your physical and mental energy levels. You will have to learn steps and styles quickly, retaining the energy and repeating the same scene many times over.

Professional dancers may choose to specialise in one dance form, such as classical ballet, contemporary dance or modern street dance. Gaps between jobs are common and many dancers combine performing with related work such as teaching or working on community projects.

Entry qualifications

If you are considering a career in dance you should be aware of the limitations of a dance degree, especially as preparation for performance. While you'll dance on most dance degree courses, degree studies in the subject do not offer the extent of specialist performance training provided by a CDET-accredited school. Dance degree graduates often enter arts administration and management, teaching, the health and leisure industry, or a completely unrelated career.

Dancers usually start training at a very early age, for example taking tap or ballet classes. Dance courses are available at specialist schools and colleges such as Bird College, the Arts Educational School, Laine Theatre Arts, Performers College etc, which cater for young people from the age of ten. You can undertake full-time professional training from the age of 16, leading to various dance qualifications. CDET-accredited schools offer courses covering the disciplines of classical ballet, musical theatre and contemporary dance. Courses are full time for three years.

Training and career development

You'll need to maintain your stamina and fitness by attending regular dance or fitness classes throughout your career. Training continues throughout a dance career and even the most experienced practitioners attend regular classes and courses to update their skills or to retrain for another area of the dance profession.

In order to increase your employability you may wish to gain further training and qualifications. Some dancers take further training in dance performance, or take a qualification in an area related to performance such as community theatre work, choreography, scenography or arts administration.

You may choose to go into teaching and take a training course that qualifies you to teach privately, in recreational classes, or in a professional dance school. If you want to teach in state schools, you will need a postgraduate teaching qualification.

Some dancers undertake further training to work as dance movement therapists, yoga teachers, Alexander technique teachers or fitness coaches. Others may choose to start their own dance groups or companies.

As a dancer's working life can be relatively short and injuries can occur, so having a second career plan is advisable. Dancers' Career Development (DCD) offers advice and funding to professional dancers who are coming to the end of their performing career.

Finding vacancies

As a dancer you may be self-employed, employed on a short-term contract, or employed on a permanent contract. You could work for a UK dance company, a musical theatre or opera production company, or a television/film production company. There are also opportunities within community dance or dance education companies.

You can look for audition notices in publication such as *The Stage*, *Dancing Times* and *Variety*. You'll need to constantly promote yourself, network and, above all, perform well at auditions. Dancers often find work through networking and making contacts in the industry. Competition for work is fierce and success depends on a combination of talent, experience, contacts, determination and luck.

Stage management

Stage managers and their assistants are responsible to the director for the smooth running of rehearsals and performances. They ensure that everything and everyone, from props and scenery to actors and technical staff, is in the right place at the right time. They obtain props and furniture, and organise lighting, sound effects, microphones, prompting and set changes.

As a stage manager your tasks may involve:

- drawing up the initial props list and set requirements list

- working within the available budget
- preparing the prompt copy of the script, noting set changes, technicians' cues and actors' moves
- overseeing the installation of the set, lighting and sound
- dealing with problems quickly during performances
- responsibility for stage safety.

Stage managers often work in the theatre all day, and stay until the lights go out after the evening performance. The equivalent job in television is a floor manager, and in films an assistant director. There is no equivalent in radio.

Entry qualifications

Many stage managers have a degree and useful subjects are stage management, theatre production, technical theatre, drama and music. Several drama schools also offer degree courses in stage management and technical theatre, which are accredited by the NCDT. Practical experience of performing, or as backstage crew, is valuable.

To be a stage manager you'll need to have excellent communication and people skills, be well organised, have financial management, administrative and IT skills, as well as stamina.

Training and career development

Many people start their career as an assistant and train on the job. You may start as a casual stage crew member, dresser, follow spot operator, acting assistant stage manager, or understudy. You may progress to assistant stage manager, deputy stage manager and finally stage manager. A career in stage management may provide opportunities to move into film or television production, theatre administration or events management.

The Stage Management Association (SMA), the UK membership organisation for stage managers, runs short, practical training courses.

Finding vacancies

Many posts are gained through personal contacts in the industry. Many stage managers are self-employed and work on short-term contracts. Vacancies are advertised in specialist publications, such as *The Stage*, and on specialist websites such as www.getintotheatre.org.uk.

Sources of further information

Access to Music Ltd – tel: 0116 242 6888. www.accesstomusic.co.uk

Arts Council England – tel: 0845 300 6200. www.artscouncil.org.uk

Arts Council of Wales – tel: 0845 8734 900. www.artswales.org.uk

Associated Board of the Royal Schools of Music (ABRSM) –
tel: 0207 636 5400. www.abrsm.org

Association of British Orchestras – tel: 020 7287 0333.
www.abo.org.uk

Association of Professional Music Therapists – tel: 020 7837 6100.
www.apmt.org

British Recorded Music Industry (BPI) (the Music Education Directory,
a free annual guide to music-focused courses in the UK, is available on
its website) – tel: 020 7803 1300. www.bpi-med.co.uk

Conference of Drama Schools – www.drama.ac.uk

Council for Dance Education and Training – tel: 020 7240 5703.
www.cdet.org.uk

Creative & Cultural Skills – the Sector Skills Council for advertising,
crafts, cultural heritage, design, literature, music, performing and visual
arts. Tel: 020 7015 1800. www.ccskills.org.uk and
www.creative-choices.co.uk

Dance UK – tel: 0207 7130 730. www.danceuk.org

Equity – tel: 0207 379 6000. www.equity.org.uk

Incorporated Society of Musicians – tel: 020 7629 4413.
www.ism.org

Musicians' Union – tel: 020 7840 5504. www.musiciansunion.org.uk

National Council of Drama Training – tel: 0207 407 3686.
www.ncdt.co.uk

Section 3
Other careers you could consider

Chapter thirteen

Careers in education

This chapter covers teaching:

- in state schools
- in further education
- in higher education
- English to speakers of other languages.

Although teaching can be challenging, the emotional rewards can be huge. It takes imagination, confidence and communication skills to help others achieve their potential. In general, teachers specialise in teaching subjects closely linked to the subject of their degree. However, it is also possible to train to teach other, unrelated, subjects, depending on the type of work you go into.

Teachers have many duties alongside taking lessons, such as planning, preparation and assessment. In order to ensure students are supported effectively, teachers attend meetings and liaise with other interested parties, such as teaching colleagues, other professionals and parents. There is also a considerable amount of record keeping required of each student's learning and progress. New initiatives and developments in particular subjects mean that teachers must undergo continuous professional development (CPD) to keep up to date.

Teaching in state schools

Primary teachers work with pupils from the age of four or five up to eleven. They teach the subjects that are set out in the National Curriculum, but focus a great deal on developing pupils' literacy (reading, writing, listening and speaking) and numeracy (number skills, mental arithmetic and so on). Teaching at primary level requires a great deal of enthusiasm and creativity, and the ability to adapt your teaching style to varying ability levels. Teachers often take on a carer's role, tending minor ills and sorting out children's problems.

Secondary teachers are usually specialists in one or two subjects from the National Curriculum. Schools may also offer subjects outside the National Curriculum as GCSE, AS/A level or Diploma options, such as leisure and tourism, engineering, manufacturing and product design. Secondary teachers may be required to take on a tutorial role and be involved in the delivery of personal, social, health and economic education (PSHE).

Financial incentives are available to those training to teach those subjects where there are teacher shortages. In recent times, there has been a shortage of teachers in maths, physics, chemistry and modern languages.

Entry qualifications

Your degree needs to be in a subject relevant to the National Curriculum. You also need GCSEs in English and maths at grades A*-C (or equivalent qualifications). If you wish to train as a primary teacher, you also need a GCSE in science at grade A*-C (or equivalent).

An empathy with children and a patient, tolerant and sensitive approach, are obviously important personal qualities required by teachers. Good communication and listening skills, and a sound knowledge of your subject(s) are essential. For primary teaching, in particular, a wide range of abilities and interests may be beneficial, such as in arts and crafts, sport, music or drama.

If you are considering a career in teaching, it is essential that you gain classroom experience before applying for training, so that you can show an understanding of the teacher's role. Contact the Training and Development Agency for Schools (TDA) for advice about how you can gain relevant work experience.

Before starting your training, you will need to undergo checks on your suitability to teach (including criminal record, background, health, identity and employment checks).

Training and career development

To teach in a state school, you need to follow initial teacher training (ITT) leading to Qualified Teacher Status (QTS). After which you must complete an induction period and then register with the appropriate

General Teaching Council (GTC) depending on which part of the country you work in. During your training, you specialise in teaching pupils of a particular age range.

Graduates can train to become teachers by taking a postgraduate course (PGCE) or an employment-based route, as described below.

Universities and colleges offer one-year, full-time courses leading to a **PGCE** (which stands for both the Postgraduate Certificate in Education and the Professional Graduate Certificate in Education). The Professional Certificate is at honours-degree level, while the Postgraduate Certificate is academically more demanding. Both types of PGCE aim to develop your teaching skills by combining classroom practice with academic study. There are also some part-time, flexible- and distance-learning routes.

Alternatively, training for a PGCE may be through a group of schools that offer SCITT (school-centred initial teacher training). This involves more time in the classroom and is usually taught by practising teachers.

There are special courses for people who need to boost their subject knowledge – particularly in shortage subjects. Contact the TDA for further details.

Employment-based training routes include the Graduate Teacher Programme (GTP), and Teach First. These offer graduates the chance to work, and earn a salary, as unqualified teachers, while receiving much of their training in school.

Qualified teachers can look to develop their careers in a number of ways. Staying within the classroom, it may be possible to train as a special educational needs (SEN) teacher or as an advanced skills teacher. There are opportunities to move into school management, ultimately to the level of headteacher. Experienced teachers can also consider roles in the wider educational field, such as a teacher trainer; Ofsted inspector; education officer for a museum, zoo, etc; adviser for a local authority education department, exam board or educational charity; and so on.

Finding vacancies

Applications for PGCEs are usually made through the Graduate Teacher Training Registry (GTTR). Alternatively, some SCITT providers accept direct applications. The TDA website has further information.

To apply for the GTP you usually need to find a school willing to employ you before applying to your local GTP training provider. You can search for details of employing schools and training providers in your area via the TDA website. Teach First operates an online recruitment system via a dedicated website (see below).

General teaching vacancies may be advertised by local authorities via their regular bulletins or on their websites, on the official recruitment website for local government jobs (www.LGjobs.com), on schools' own websites, or every Friday in the *Times Educational Supplement.*

While at university, or as a recent graduate, you can access information about potential employers and current graduate vacancies through your university careers service. Further information about the help available through university careers services is provided in Chapter three.

Sources of further information

General Teaching Council for England – tel: 0870 001 0308. www.gtce.org.uk
General Teaching Council for Wales – tel: 029 2055 0350. www.gtcw.org.uk
Graduate Teacher Training Registry (GTTR) – tel: 0871 468 0469. www.gttr.ac.uk
Teach First – tel: 0844 880 1800. www.teachfirst.org.uk
Teacher Training & Education in Wales – www.teachertrainingwales.org

Training and Development Agency for Schools (TDA) – tel: 0845 6000 991 (or 0845 6000 922 for Welsh speakers). www.tda.gov.uk

Teaching in further education

The majority of further education (FE) takes place in FE and sixth-form colleges and is aimed at students aged between 16 and 19. However, FE may also refer to education provided in adult and community learning, work-based learning and offender-learning settings.

Teachers in FE deliver a huge variety of subjects and qualifications, such as:

- vocational courses in subjects such as media and performing arts

- GCSEs and A levels

- Access courses for people who want to go on to higher education (HE)

- some HE courses – foundation degrees, HNCs, HNDs and degrees

- courses leading to qualifications from professional bodies.

Alongside all the typical work of a teacher, FE teachers are likely to be involved in recruiting and selecting students for their courses, acting as a personal tutor, and fostering strong links with local employers. The work may involve teaching evening classes and classes during college holidays.

There are two teaching roles within FE: **full teacher** (has the full range of teaching responsibilities, including developing the curriculum and planning how it will be taught) and **associate teacher** (has fewer responsibilities; for example, may teach from a pre-prepared pack). To work in either role, you need a qualification endorsed by Standards Verification UK (SVUK).

Entry qualifications

Depending on the courses you intend to teach, you will need professional or academic qualifications in those areas, and relevant business/industrial experience for work-related subjects. With a degree, it is possible to teach academic subjects at least up to A level.

Obviously, a thorough and up-to-date knowledge of your subject is essential for this type of work; you will also need strong communication and organisation skills, flexibility and enthusiasm for teaching people from a wide range of backgrounds.

You need to undergo background checks if you intend to work with children, young people or vulnerable adults.

Training and career development

To qualify as an associate teacher, you need to complete the Certificate in Teaching in the Lifelong Learning Sector (CTLLS). Courses leading to the CTLLS are usually offered on a part-time basis, and are aimed at those already employed in the FE sector. Following this, you need to complete a period of assessed work experience known as professional formation. On completion, you can apply for Associate Teacher Learning and Skills (ATLS) status.

Full teachers have the option of completing either of the following:

- the Diploma in Teaching in the Lifelong Learning Sector (DTLLS)

- the Postgraduate Certificate in Education (PGCE) Post-Compulsory Education and Training (PCET).

These qualifications can either be taken prior to employment in the sector, as a one-year, full-time course or, if you already have a teaching post, as a two-year, part-time course.

Following this, you need to complete your professional formation. On completion, you can apply for Qualified Teacher Learning and Skills (QTLS) status.

FE teachers need to be registered with the Institute for Learning (IfL).

N.B. In Wales, there is currently no equivalent requirement to ATLS/QTLS, but there may be in the future. To teach in an FE college in Wales, you need to have or gain a teaching qualification that is endorsed by SVUK. For more information, contact Lifelong Learning UK (LLUK) – the Sector Skills Council covering FE education.

Finding vacancies

Vacancies are advertised on the Association of Colleges' website, and on websites of individual colleges. Vacancies are also listed every Friday in the *Times Educational Supplement.*

While at university, or as a recent graduate, you can access information about potential employers and current graduate vacancies through your university careers service. Further information about the help available through university careers services is provided in Chapter three.

Sources of further information

Association of Colleges – tel: 020 7299 6980. www.aoc.co.uk

Institute for Learning (IfL) – tel: 0844 815 3202. www.ifl.ac.uk

Lifelong Learning UK (LLUK) – tel: 0300 303 1877. www.lluk.org

Standards Verification UK (SVUK) – tel: 0113 241 0427. www.standardsverificationuk.org

Teaching in higher education

Teaching in higher education (HE) is often combined with research. This research may be purely academic, or it may be sponsored by industry to solve practical problems. Teaching can involve one-to-one tutorials, group seminars of, say, 10 to 20 students, or lectures that may be given to groups of anything from 25 to a few hundred students. 'Virtual' lectures are sometimes given via the internet.

Subjects taught at HE level include traditional academic subjects, such as English or history, as well as work-related subjects, such as public relations or landscape architecture. HE institutions may also offer courses leading to professional qualifications. Subjects are also taught at postgraduate level.

Entry qualifications

You will be teaching very able students who already have level 3 qualifications (A levels, Advanced Diplomas, etc), so you need to be highly qualified in your subject area – typically with a good honours degree, plus a masters degree or, preferably, a PhD.

Training and career development

Many lecturers start out as postgraduate research assistants or teaching assistants, being paid to assist while gaining their own postgraduate qualifications. This can often lead to a lecturer's post, once qualified.

Increasingly, HE institutions expect their teaching staff to undergo some formal teacher training or, at least, in-house induction and professional development programmes. This may involve a probationary period and mentoring. The quality of teaching is one of the factors looked at when HE courses and institutions are inspected.

The Higher Education Academy operates a professional recognition scheme. Experienced teaching staff, and those who have completed professional development schemes that are recognised by the academy, can achieve Associate, Fellow or Senior Fellow status. For more information, see the academy website, listed below.

University and college lecturers can be promoted to senior or principal lecturer posts, or professorships. The highest post is vice-chancellor of a university. Many academics also publish books or write articles for journals on their subject. Some, who are particularly good communicators, present radio and television programmes.

Finding vacancies

Jobs are advertised in the *THE* (*Times Higher Education*) every Friday, as well as in certain newspapers, and on the websites of individual HE institutions.

While at university, or as a recent graduate, you can access information about potential employers and current graduate vacancies through your university careers service. Further information about the help available through university careers services is provided in Chapter three.

Sources of further information

The Higher Education Academy – tel: 01904 717500.
www.heacademy.ac.uk

Teaching English to speakers of other languages

There are opportunities to work in the UK, and abroad, teaching English to speakers of other languages, generally referred to as TESOL. In the UK, you can teach English in a commercial language school, FE college, community and adult learning setting, or HE institution. Or you may be employed to provide English language support to foreign students while they are studying in the UK. Overseas, there are opportunities to teach English with commercial language schools, voluntary organisations, large employers and the British Council.

Whatever the setting, what you teach will depend on the needs of your students. They may want to be able to read, write and speak English to a high level, perhaps for business purposes. Some may just want to speak and understand the language at a basic level. In some situations, you may have contact with your students over a long period; in others, you may be teaching students on short, intensive courses. Classes are usually small, and may involve teaching on a one-to-one basis.

Entry qualifications

Recognised UK-based language schools expect teachers to be graduates and to hold a relevant English language teaching qualification. Requirements to teach overseas vary; however, most reputable employers require the same standards as UK-based language schools.

In order to teach in the FE sector in England, teachers need to have Qualified Teacher Learning and Skills (QTLS) status and be registered with the Institute for Learning. They also need a specific qualification for TESOL, which can be taken separately or as part of the DTLLS (see earlier).

N.B. These regulations do not apply to teachers in further education in Wales, where there are currently no specific minimum qualifications to teach ESOL. Employers set their own entry requirements. However, this is under review and is likely to change. For up-to-date information contact Lifelong Learning UK.

The British Council only employs graduates who have an acceptable teaching qualification and a minimum of two years' relevant experience.

Training and career development

There are a number of courses available, ranging from introductory or taster courses through to advanced-level qualifications, offered by different examining bodies at accredited centres and via distance learning. The two main organisations that award relevant qualifications are the University of Cambridge ESOL Examinations and Trinity College London.

Various postgraduate courses offered by universities and other HE institutions provide specialist study in, or relevant to, TESOL. These vary so much that the syllabus of each should be examined carefully to see whether the content is really relevant to your particular requirements.

Although opportunities for promotion are limited in this line of work, there may be opportunities to move into a managerial position in a large school or college. You could also think about specialising, for example in teaching business English. Self-employment is an option – you could set up your own language school or undertake private tuition.

Finding vacancies

Vacancies are advertised on the online version of *EL Gazette*, as well as on many general online job sites.

While at university, or as a recent graduate, you can access information about potential employers and current graduate vacancies through your university careers service. Further information about the help available through university careers services is provided in Chapter three.

Sources of further information

British Council Information Centre – tel: 0161 957 7755. www.britishcouncil.org/teacherrecruitment

English UK – association of over 400 providers of English language teaching in Britain that are accredited by the British Council. Tel: 020 7608 7960. www.englishuk.com

International House London – a major employer of teachers in its language schools overseas, and a teacher training provider. Tel: 020 7611 2400. www.ihlondon.com

Trinity College London – tel: 020 7820 6100. www.trinitycollege.co.uk

University of Cambridge ESOL Examinations – www.cambridgeesol.org

Chapter fourteen

Careers in finance

Opportunities for financial specialists are not just limited to the financial services sector; all areas of the economy require people who can manage money, including the public sector, industry and commerce, and individuals. As a graduate you could consider working:

- as an accountant
- as an actuary
- in a bank or building society
- in insurance
- as a stockbroker.

Accountant

There are three main areas in which accountants work. Most accountants work in **private practice** (sometimes confusingly referred to as public practice), which means they are employed by an accountancy firm to provide financial services to individuals and to organisations of all types and sizes. Accountants working in **industry and commerce** offer in-house expertise for their employer's business. **Public sector** accountants work for local government, the NHS and other public services, where the emphasis is on ensuring taxpayers' money is spent as efficiently as possible. The exact nature of the work varies according to your specialism.

Financial accountants oversee the financial transactions of an organisation. This entails managing the payment of wages, taxes, invoices and so on; ensuring details of all income and expenditure are recorded; preparing the accounts and reports for directors; managing investments and protecting assets; and carrying out internal audits of the organisation's financial affairs.

Management accountants collect and analyse an organisation's financial information in order to forecast results, create business plans, control budgets, perform cost/benefit analysis of future projects and prepare management reports. In effect, they act as internal consultants specialising in the financial performance of the organisation.

Auditors examine accounts that others have prepared to check that they are a 'true and fair view' of the organisation's affairs. This involves interviewing staff at all levels and checking supporting documents to find out how the data was compiled, what policies are in place and how they are enforced. Internal auditors look at the accounts of the organisation they work for and offer advice on best practice. External auditors can either work for private firms that audit company accounts for clients or public sector organisations such as the Audit Commission or the National Audit Office, which seek to ensure that local and central government, the NHS, etc provide good value for money.

Accountants can specialise in many other areas relating to finance. For example, **taxation specialists** provide advice to individuals and organisations about their tax status and liabilities and negotiate tax assessments with HM Revenue & Customs (HMRC). **Insolvency specialists** work with failing businesses to guide them through the winding-up process – selling off assets and paying creditors. **Corporate finance specialists** support companies involved in mergers and acquisitions, by producing business plans and financial projections, as well as advising on methods of raising the necessary finance.

Entry qualifications

Training leading to chartered status is through one of the professional accountancy bodies, which include:

- the Institute of Chartered Accountants in England and Wales (ICAEW)
- the Association of Chartered Certified Accountants (ACCA)
- the Chartered Institute of Management Accountants (CIMA)
- the Chartered Institute of Public Finance and Accountancy (CIPFA).

To qualify you need to pass professional exams and undertake a period of practical experience. Although a degree is not required by the accountancy bodies to begin training, in practice, many accountants are graduates and employers offering training contracts may require at least a 2:1 degree for entry. In addition, you are normally expected to have a strong academic track record at GCSE and A level (or equivalent).

As you would expect, accountants need a good level of numeracy, ICT skills and the ability to analyse information, but must also be able to communicate complex ideas to non-specialists and have a logical mind and an interest in business.

Training and career development

The professional accountancy bodies offer several routes to qualifying, including training on the job, part- or full-time college courses, and distance learning. Training can take three to four years, including relevant work experience. Note that qualifying as a chartered accountant involves a level of study equivalent to taking another degree, usually while doing a full-time job! All accountants are expected to take part in continuing professional development (CPD) throughout their careers.

Training for an accountancy qualification is excellent preparation for a general management career in almost any area of the economy. For example, while it is not a prerequisite, many company directors, chief executives and company secretaries first trained as accountants. In the public sector, accountants can progress to the level of chief financial officer or treasurer of a local authority, for example. In private practice, it is possible to become a partner of a firm of accountants or be self-employed. Accountancy training can also be good preparation for someone who wants to start to run any other type of enterprise, because it can develop both business awareness and knowledge of financial management.

Finding vacancies

Vacancies are advertised on the websites of the professional accountancy bodies, by specialist recruitment agencies, on many specialist and general online job sites, in publications such as *Accountancy* and *Accountancy Age*, in the appointments sections of certain daily newspapers and on employers' own websites.

While at university, or as a recent graduate, you can access information about potential employers and current graduate vacancies through your university careers service. Further information about the help available through university careers services is provided in Chapter three.

Sources of further information

Association of Chartered Certified Accountants (ACCA) – tel: 020 7059 5000. www.accaglobal.com

Association of International Accountants (AIA) – tel: 0191 493 0277. www.aiaworldwide.com

Audit Commission – tel: 0844 798 1212. www.everybody-counts.co.uk and www.whatisyouraudit.com

Chartered Institute of Management Accountants (CIMA) – tel: 020 8849 2251. www.cimaglobal.com

Chartered Institute of Public Finance & Accountancy (CIPFA) – tel: 020 7543 5600. www.cipfa.org.uk

Institute of Chartered Accountants in England and Wales (ICAEW) – tel: 01908 248040. www.icaew.com

Institute of Financial Accountants (IFA) – tel: 01732 458080. www.ifa.org.uk

National Audit Office – tel: 020 7798 7227. www.nao.org.uk

Actuary

Actuaries calculate risks – the probability of certain things happening – and then apply their findings to financial problems, such as how much people should pay for life insurance or into their pensions. Statistics and probability theory are the basis of much of their work.

Actuaries are employed in many areas of the financial sector, including insurance, investment, pensions and specialist consultancy. Some work in the public sector for the Government Actuary's Department (GAD), which advises the UK government, and other countries, on pensions policy and regulation, social security benefits, occupational pensions, insurance and so on.

Entry qualifications

Most entrants to the profession have a degree in a numerate subject, although it is possible for graduates who have a first- or second-class degree in any subject to go into actuarial work provided they can demonstrate a high level of numeracy, such as through an A level in maths at grade A*-C. The Actuarial Profession (an organisation that represents the professional actuarial bodies covering England, Wales and Scotland) offers a Certificate in financial mathematics, suitable for undergraduates who want to enhance their career prospects in the finance sector.

While mathematical ability is clearly required, actuaries must also be able to communicate clearly to non-specialists, both orally and in writing.

Training and career development

To qualify as an actuary in England and Wales, you must pass the professional exams of the Institute of Actuaries while working in a suitable training position. It can take between three and six years to qualify. Tuition for the exams is by the Actuarial Education Company and usually combines distance learning and personal tuition. Your path is made easier if you undertake a postgraduate course in actuarial science as this, as well as relevant degrees, can earn exemptions from some of the professional examinations.

Actuaries can move out of specific actuarial work into middle and senior management, especially in life insurance companies and pension funds.

Finding vacancies

Vacancies are advertised in *The Actuary*, published monthly, and on its associated website, www.the-actuary.org.uk. A list of actuarial employers can be found on the website of the Actuarial Profession. Vacancies are also advertised by specialist recruitment agencies, on many specialist and general online job sites, and in the appointments sections of certain daily newspapers.

While at university, or as a recent graduate, you can access information about potential employers and current graduate vacancies through your university careers service. Further information about the help that is available through university careers services is provided in Chapter three.

Sources of further information

The Actuarial Profession – incorporates the Institute of Actuaries. Tel: 020 7632 2100. www.actuaries.org.uk

Banks and building societies

Retail banks and building societies provide many of the same financial services – they offer current accounts and savings accounts; lend money and issue credit cards; clear cheques and transfer funds; invest money; buy and sell foreign currency; and sell a range of 'financial products' to individuals and organisations. The main difference between them is that retail banks are owned by shareholders, while building societies are owned by their members – the people who deposit money with them or who take out mortgages from them.

Managers in retail banks and building societies are responsible for the day-to-day running of a branch, a region of branches or a specialist department at headquarters. They must attract business to the organisation by offering financial products and services that customers want, while at the same time managing risk, for example, by assessing the credit-worthiness of individuals or firms. Within a branch, they manage and train the customer services team and spend a lot of time visiting businesses – discussing their business plans, loans, insurance and other needs. Within head office, there are opportunities to specialise in financial legal work (such as compliance), ICT, marketing, insurance, investment management, human resources and training, and financial administration.

Investment banks, also known as corporate or merchant banks, provide services similar to the retail banks but to customers that range from small businesses to multinational corporations and overseas governments. As well as taking deposits, making loans and transferring funds, their work includes financing international trade, advising on mergers and takeovers, and raising capital. They buy and sell foreign currency and manage pension funds and investment trusts. They help companies acquire assets, such as a fleet of new lorries, by buying them and leasing them to the customer. They are also involved in floating companies on the stock market and buying and selling shares.

The Bank of England acts as banker to the Government and to the other banks. It is responsible for issuing and destroying banknotes, setting interest rates, and has responsibilities for other institutions in the money and foreign exchange markets. It has a key role in government financial policies and is vital to the functioning of the economy. Much of its work involves the collection, analysis and interpretation of economic and financial data relating both to the British economy and to economic conditions abroad.

Most retail banks have large **international banking** divisions, with operations in the major financial centres of the world. Similarly, many overseas banks have branches in the UK, particularly London. Staff are usually recruited from the local area and normally only very senior staff get the opportunity to work abroad. International banking careers therefore involve working in this country, but specialising in foreign exchange, shipping documents, foreign stocks and shares etc. As well as the direct banking careers, there are openings in specialist roles such as audit, accountancy, actuarial work and ICT.

Entry qualifications

Management trainee schemes offered by retail banks, building societies and investment banks usually require at least a second-class degree in any subject for entry. The Bank of England requires at least a 2:1, plus a minimum of 300 UCAS Tariff points at A level (or equivalent) for entry onto its graduate scheme, known as the Analyst Career Training (ACT) programme. Because most banks and building societies have large branch networks, you are normally required to be mobile and able to lead a team. Good communication and ICT skills are also essential.

Training and career development

Graduate training schemes combine work experience in a variety of functions with a programme of study. These studies lead to professional qualifications, such as those offered by the *ifs* School of Finance. Progress within the banking sector depends on your performance. You may move up in management roles of increasing seniority or become a specialist in a particular area.

Finding vacancies

Employers advertise details of their graduate training schemes on their own websites. Vacancies are also advertised by specialist recruitment agencies, on many specialist and general online job sites, and in the appointments sections of certain daily newspapers.

While at university, or as a recent graduate, you can access information about potential employers and current graduate vacancies through your university careers service. Further information about the help available through university careers services is provided in Chapter three.

Sources of further information

Bank of England – tel: 020 7601 4444. www.bankofenglandjobs.co.uk

Barclays Bank – tel: 0845 241 4936. www.barclays-graduates.co.uk

Britannia Building Society – www.britannia.co.uk

The Building Societies Association – tel: 020 7520 5900. www.bsa.org.uk

Financial Services Skills Council – the Sector Skills Council for financial services, accountancy and finance. Tel: 0845 257 3772. www.fssc.org.uk

HSBC – http://jobs.hsbc.co.uk/graduates

ifs **School of Finance** – tel: 01227 818609. www.ifslearning.ac.uk

Lloyds Banking Group (which includes Lloyds TSB, Halifax and Bank of Scotland) – www.lloydsbankinggrouptalent.com

Nationwide – www.nationwide-jobs.co.uk

RBS (The Royal Bank of Scotland Group, which includes NatWest) – www.makeitrbs.com

Santander – www.santanderukgraduates.com

Insurance

Insurance is a way of protecting people from losses arising from sickness, theft, fire, accident and other misfortunes. Insurance is based on the laws of probability: that is, the likelihood of certain events occurring or happening to people. The principle behind it is that many people regularly pay into a common fund but only a few people will need to claim compensation for a loss.

The insurance sector in the UK comprises:

- several hundred insurance companies – some specialise in particular areas such as vehicle, marine, commercial, health or aviation, while others provide a wide range of services

- insurance brokers – who act as intermediaries between the customer and the insurer to help customers find the best policies, often negotiating on their behalf

- the famous Lloyd's of London – which is an insurance 'market' where the insurance cover, usually for large-scale risks, is provided by syndicates of individuals.

Underwriters, both in the insurance companies and those in Lloyd's, are responsible for calculating the risks, deciding whether they are insurable and, if so, on what terms. Some risks are simple to assess and are based on standard guidelines. Others, such as for the Olympic Games or a space satellite, are more complex and unique. It is here that the specialist skills of an underwriter are required to work out premiums and the terms and conditions of the policy. Technical advice may be provided by insurance surveyors.

Insurance surveyors visit the commercial site or property that is to be insured and report on any aspects that might affect the underwriter's assessment, such as the use of dangerous materials, fire risks and security. Surveyors also advise clients on how to reduce their risks (and so their premiums) through improved security, safer storage of flammable materials and so on. The work may also include carrying out surveys of ships, aircraft, etc. The work of an insurance surveyor can include a large amount of travel, possibly including overseas. Insurance surveyors are often drawn from existing staff and given appropriate training.

When claims are made, claims staff assess the loss and decide the amount to be paid. Some claim assessments are quite simple and will be handled by **claims technicians**. Others may require the intervention of **claims negotiators** who have expert knowledge in a particular area such as law or medicine. The claims negotiator may need to visit the site of the claim, interview witnesses and inspect damage before deciding on the outcome of the claim. For large, complex or disputed claims, the insurer may bring in a **loss adjuster** to examine the claim and help to reach a settlement. The insured party may also employ their own independent loss adjuster to negotiate the claim on their behalf.

Insurance agents are authorised by insurance companies to sell a wide range of insurance products on their behalf to the general public and to brokers. **Brokers** are experts in insurance and help their clients to choose and buy the best insurance policy to meet their needs. They earn commission from the insurer once a policy has been bought and may be self-employed or work for large firms of brokers. Brokers must have a wide knowledge of the insurance market, insurance law and practice. Although their main function is to get the best type of cover for their clients, they may also advise on how to lessen risks by improving fire precautions, isolating dangerous materials and so on.

Entry qualifications

Usually, any degree subject is acceptable for entry onto graduate training schemes, although mathematical and business-related disciplines are particularly relevant. You need to be numerate, have an analytical mind and be able to combine assertiveness with tact (you may have to deal sensitively with people who have suffered various calamities). You must be a persuasive communicator, both orally and in writing.

Training and career development

Your training is likely to combine on-the-job work experience, in a variety of functions, with part-time study. The main professional body that offers qualifications in insurance is the Chartered Insurance Institute (CII). To gain chartered status as an insurer, insurance practitioner or insurance broker, you need at least five years' relevant work experience and to have passed a CII-approved qualification, such as the Advanced Diploma in Insurance. You also need to commit to an ongoing programme of continuing professional development (CPD).

Finding vacancies

Employers advertise details of their graduate training schemes on their own websites. Vacancies are also advertised by specialist recruitment agencies, on many specialist and general online job sites, and in the appointments sections of certain daily newspapers.

While at university, or as a recent graduate, you can access information about potential employers and current graduate vacancies through your university careers service. Further information about the help available through university careers services is provided in Chapter three.

Sources of further information

The Chartered Insurance Institute (CII) – tel: 020 8989 8464. www.cii.co.uk

The Chartered Institute of Loss Adjusters – tel: 020 7337 9960. www.cila.co.uk

Financial Services Skills Council – the Sector Skills Council for financial services, accountancy and finance. Tel: 0845 257 3772. www.fssc.org.uk

Lloyds – tel: 020 7327 1000. www.lloyds.com

Stockbroking

The London Stock Exchange is a marketplace where companies can raise money by issuing and selling shares to individual and institutional investors. The Government also raises money there by selling bonds. Many individuals buy stocks and shares, many more have investments made on their behalf by the banks, building societies, pension funds and others who hold their money.

Stockbrokers, also known as dealers, advise clients, buy and sell stocks and shares on their behalf, and help clients manage their investments. They need to research the stock market and take advice from investment analysts, as well as regularly reviewing the performance of their clients' portfolios. Most contact with clients is carried out over the phone or by letter, while trading is done mainly over the phone or internet. Stockbrokers work long hours in a high-pressure environment. Firms of stockbrokers range from small firms to large international securities houses with hundreds of employees.

Market makers, also known as traders, are stockbrokers who act like wholesalers within the stock market by buying and selling stocks and shares on behalf of their own firm. They speculate on the potential supply and demand of particular shares, with the aim of selling the shares they buy at a profit. This involves researching the financial press and other sources of market information, consulting investment analysts and deciding the selling price of their shares. It's a high-pressured role that needs sound judgement and the ability to make quick decisions.

Other specialist roles relating to the stock market include those working in: corporate finance – raising finance for companies by issuing new shares; mergers and acquisitions – advising client companies and arranging finance for such activities; and **fund management** – managing investments for institutional clients. There are also openings to become **investment analysts** or **researchers**. These are specialists who provide market intelligence to brokers, market makers and institutional investors.

Entry qualifications

Any degree subject may be acceptable. However, arts and humanities graduates should be aware that, for some roles, employers prefer degrees with a high mathematical content. A background in law, economics, finance or business would also be useful. Alternatively, analysts may have degrees related to the area in which they want to specialise, for example, surveying for property analysts.

Regardless of which area of work you enter, you will need to be numerate, articulate and able to assimilate lots of data quickly and accurately. You must have a good analytical mind and plenty of stamina. You should also be interested in current affairs. Above all, you must have the social skills necessary if you are to form good relationships with clients and earn their confidence.

Training and career development

A graduate training programme is likely to combine classroom training with on-the-job experience. Many roles in this sector are regulated by the Financial Services Authority (FSA), which means to work unsupervised you must have passed an 'appropriate' exam as detailed by the FSSC (the Financial Services Skills Council). Even in unregulated roles, for example in compliance (which involves ensuring the organisation and its employees comply with all relevant regulations), employers are still likely to expect you to gain a qualification from the FSSC's 'recommended' exam list. The Chartered Institute for Securities and Investment (CISI) is the main professional body for this sector and offers relevant exams, as does the CFA Society of the UK.

Finding vacancies

Contact the London Stock Exchange for details of member firms who are likely to advertise vacancies, and details of any graduate training schemes they run on their own websites. The CISI website also lists a selection of graduate schemes as well as career events. Vacancies are also advertised by specialist recruitment agencies, on many specialist and general online job sites, and in the appointments sections of certain daily newspapers.

While at university, or as a recent graduate, you can access information about potential employers and current graduate vacancies through your university careers service. Further information about the help that is available through university careers services is provided in Chapter three.

Sources of further information

Chartered Institute for Securities & Investment (CISI) – tel: 020 7645 0600. www.cisi.org

CFA Society of the UK – tel: 020 7280 9620. www.cfauk.org

Financial Services Skills Council – the Sector Skills Council for financial services, accountancy and finance. Tel: 0845 257 3772. www.fssc.org.uk

The London Stock Exchange – tel: 020 7797 1000. www.londonstockexchange.com

Chapter fifteen

Careers in leisure, travel and tourism

Although the leisure, travel and tourism sector offers plenty of openings, few of the jobs are exclusively for graduates. You can expect to compete for jobs with non-graduates with relevant work experience. However, you should find that the transferable skills acquired during your degree studies help to give you an advantage. Some of the larger employers do recruit graduates specifically, and run graduate training programmes.

This chapter briefly describes the following careers:

- arts administrator
- catering manager
- conference and exhibition manager
- entertainments manager
- events manager
- hotel manager
- tour operator and related work
- tourism officer
- visitor attraction/holiday centre manager.

Arts administrator

Arts administrators organise events such as concerts, plays, art exhibitions and festivals. Employers may be theatre and dance companies, community arts organisations and local authorities. The responsibilities of the job include:

- planning seasonal programmes
- organising individual events

- booking venues
- engaging performers
- publicity
- negotiating grants from public funds and commercial sponsorship
- day-to-day administration.

The exact nature of the work will depend largely on the size of the organisation for which you work. For example, in a large organisation you might specialise in marketing, whereas in a small organisation you could be responsible for all the activities listed above.

Catering manager

Catering managers have to plan, organise and manage food and beverage services. They are mainly employed by hotels, restaurants, businesses, hospitals, care homes, cruise ships, holiday centres, educational institutions, conference centres and other places where large numbers of people need to eat and drink. Catering managers have to achieve customer satisfaction while balancing quality and cost. They are also responsible for maintaining high standards of cleanliness and food hygiene. Many graduates who go into catering management have gained relevant experience through doing part-time or seasonal jobs at weekends and during university vacations.

Conference and exhibition manager

Exhibition and conference centres, and some larger hotels, employ managers to organise and direct all the appropriate services for the running of events. These can range from one-day events involving a few dozen delegates to events attended by several thousand people over three or four days. The latter may combine an exhibition with a programme of workshops, lectures and other meetings.

The manager has overall responsibility for ensuring that all the services run smoothly - delegate reception, accommodation and catering, lecture rooms and their seating, exhibitions, audiovisual equipment, press office, entertainment and so on. The manager leads a team of people, but will have overall responsibility for planning, for ensuring that everything runs smoothly (and that problems are resolved satisfactorily as they arise) and that the event is profitable.

Entertainments manager

Entertainments managers are employed by organisations such as holiday centre operators, cruise companies, hotel and leisure businesses, and local authorities. The work involves organising and delivering a range of entertainments, which, depending on the setting, could include children's activities, games nights, quizzes, discos, cabarets and stage shows. Duties may include booking performers and organising individual events, dealing with publicity, managing the finances, and taking responsibility for matters such as health and safety.

Events manager

Events managers are the people that take responsibility for organising anything from festivals or outdoor concerts to horticultural shows, sporting events, weddings, private parties, charity fundraising balls or corporate hospitality functions. They mainly work for specialist events management companies.

The responsibilities of events managers are wide. They may include finding a suitable venue, sorting out advertising and publicity, making sure that legal regulations are met, negotiating with contractors and suppliers (such as staging suppliers or caterers), dealing with security and car parking, and looking after the finances.

Hotel manager

As a hotel manager you would be responsible for running every aspect of a hotel. This includes managing staff; organising the furnishings, maintenance and cleaning services; the running of the restaurant, bars and the reception area; dealing with customer complaints and unexpected problems; and, above all, being responsible for the financial performance of the business. In a large hotel you would have a management team with several heads of departments. In a small hotel you would carry out all the management tasks and even give a helping hand if any staff were absent.

Tour operator and related work

The larger tour operators recruit graduates for head office functions. Vacancies are mainly in marketing, information technology, sales, finance and contracting. Working in head office in the job role of contractor, for example, you would have to choose resorts, and negotiate with airlines, coach companies, hotels and villa owners, getting the best possible prices for your company. Finance is critical to the success of a travel company, because profit margins are normally very low for package holidays and budgets must be monitored very closely. Apart from the large, well known travel companies, there may also be opportunities with the smaller, specialist tour operators.

To gain some relevant experience, you might choose to be a **travel courier** for a season or two. As a courier you look after holiday travellers, usually while travelling by coach. You care for your party throughout the trip – welcome them, give a commentary on places of interest during the tour, liaise with hotels and restaurants, deal with problems and emergencies as they arise, and generally ensure that your clients have a trouble-free and enjoyable trip.

Another option that will provide experience is to work for a tour operator as a **resort representative** (often known as 'reps'). They do similar work to couriers but are based in a resort, where they are likely to look after clients in several hotels, dealing with problems and selling excursions etc. Representatives are usually employed by the season.

Tourism officer

Tourism officers are mainly employed by local authorities, but may also work for other public bodies and private organisations. They are responsible for marketing the attractions of their particular region, or their visitor attraction, with the aim of increasing visitor numbers. The work may involve running visitor services, such as tourist centres, and dealing with providers of visitor services, such as tourist attractions, hotels and tour operators. As a tourism officer, you would be responsible for strategic planning and organising new attractions, festivals, fairs and other events to attract visitors. You would also be involved in producing publicity materials, running a website, writing press releases, and possibly involved in commissioning DVD and television commercials.

On the administrative side, you would also be managing staff, and writing and presenting reports for your employer.

Visitor attraction/holiday centre manager

Visitor attractions, ranging from theme parks and heritage centres to holiday centres, all need a range of management staff. Large operations employ managers based at individual attractions, to manage the various on-site facilities, as well as at head office, to deal with overall company strategy, future planning, marketing, human resources, finances and so on. You can read more about careers that are particularly related to heritage work in Chapter ten.

Entry qualifications

As mentioned at the start of this chapter, having a degree is not essential for the jobs described in this chapter. However, some of the larger companies do run graduate recruitment programmes. If applying for graduate vacancies it may be an advantage to have an arts or humanities degree in a relevant subject to the career area, for example an arts degree for arts administration. It will also help your application if you have any relevant work experience, which will also provide you with industry contacts and a reference.

If you are competing against non-graduates, as a graduate you should have developed a range of skills, such as communication and problem solving, that employers value. Again, any relevant work experience will help you.

For some jobs, such as conference and exhibition management, employers look for a few years' relevant prior experience. Where relevant postgraduate courses are available, it may be worth considering taking such a course prior to entry. For example, there are some postgraduate arts administration and management courses, which may help you gain entry into that area of work.

Training and career development

For some jobs, including hotel management, some larger employers run graduate training programmes, which provide structured training over one to two years. In other organisations, and in other career areas, such as arts administration, training is mainly on the job, supplemented by relevant short courses. Larger employers may offer scope for career progression within the organisation. In smaller organisations, promotion to a more senior role may require moving to a different employer.

Finding vacancies

Opportunities with local authorities can be viewed on www.LGjobs. com. Depending on your particular career area of interest, you can find vacancies advertised in magazines such as *The Stage* (www.thestage.co.uk), *Arts Professional* (www.artsprofessional. co.uk), *Travel Trade Gazette* (www.ttglive.com) and *Travel Weekly* (www.travelweekly.co.uk).

While at university, or if a recent graduate, you can access information about potential employers and current graduate vacancies through your university careers service. Further information about the help available through university careers services is provided in Chapter three.

Sources of further information

Creative & Cultural Skills – the Sector Skills Council for advertising, crafts, cultural heritage, design, literature, music, performing and visual arts. Tel: 020 7015 1800. www.ccskills.org.uk

Institute of Hospitality – the professional body for hospitality, leisure and tourism professionals. Tel: 020 8661 4900. www.instituteofhospitality.org

Institute of Travel & Tourism (ITT) – tel: 0844 499 5653. www.itt.co.uk

People 1st – the Sector Skills Council for hospitality, leisure, travel and tourism. Tel: 01895 817000. www.people1st.co.uk

Springboard UK – promotes hospitality, leisure, travel and tourism careers, and provides careers information. Tel: 020 7497 8654. www.springboarduk.net

Chapter sixteen

Careers in library and information work

We live in an age of information. Managing it, organising it, storing it and making it accessible is the task of librarians and other information specialists. Apart from paper-based material, staff working in this field deal with film, video/DVD, photographic, microfiche, audio, CD-ROM and other electronic records.

This chapter covers the jobs of:

- librarian/information manager – including information scientist

- researcher.

Librarian/Information manager

The traditional picture of a librarian is generally someone who looks after shelves of books and lends these out to borrowers. This isn't a real reflection of the job today, which should be more realistically thought of as information management.

In Britain alone, we create huge masses of information. Apart from books (novels and non-fiction), newspapers and journals, policy documents and records are produced by every government department and agency, reports are produced by businesses and other organisations, research papers are produced by academic researchers, and so on.

Such material must be managed in a way that enables data to be easily accessed when needed. Some material must be kept for years for legal, administrative, financial and other purposes. Some is of historical significance and must be retained in permanent archives. All these decisions and responsibilities fall to the librarian or information manager.

The work of librarians and information managers – who are sometimes called information specialists – is very similar. The particular responsibilities vary depending on the situation – such as looking after information resources in a reference library or a specialist library in business or industry, or for a professional body. Keeping records electronically is an increasingly important part of the work, as is managing digital cataloguing systems.

Librarians in public lending libraries are responsible for the selection, purchase, cataloguing and arrangement of books, periodicals, DVDs, CDs, information packs and other materials. Some librarians organise special services such as mobile libraries, children's activities and business sections.

Academic librarians serve both staff and students. In collaboration with their academic colleagues, they select materials to support the study and research taking place in the institution. Many academic librarians specialise in a particular subject area.

In some jobs, you may be involved in creating indexing and suitable storing systems. You may need to ensure that anyone authorised to do so can easily access the information you look after. You may have to handle internal and external requests for information.

Information scientist

This role is very similar to that of an information manager, but the emphasis of the work is often in a specialist field, such as scientific, technical, legal, economic or commercial. Information scientists may work for research organisations, professional institutions, employers, government agencies and other bodies. Besides managing the information resources and helping users locate the information they need, information scientists may develop new databases, conduct information searches and write reports, produce summaries or abstracts of information and analyse statistical information. They could also be responsible for online data services such as intranets (internal corporate websites).

Entry qualifications

Those whose first degree is not in librarianship, information management or information science will need to take a postgraduate course, accredited by the Chartered Institute of Library and Information Professionals (CILIP). Relevant work experience is often required for entry to a postgraduate course.

People working in information management need good organisational and communication skills, and to be confident with ICT.

Training and career development

Staff may work towards chartered membership of CILIP. With experience, it is possible to gain promotion to management-level roles, or move into a more specialist information role.

Finding vacancies

CILIP publishes the *Library and Information Gazette*, which carries professional-level vacancies (and can be accessed online). You can also find relevant vacancies on www.lisjobnet.com or, for local government, see www.LGtalent.com (which also carries careers information).

While at university, or if a recent graduate, you can access current graduate vacancies through your university careers service. Further details about the advice and information available through university careers services are provided in Chapter three.

Sources of further information

Aslib, The Association for Information Management – tel: 020 7253 3349. www.aslib.com

Chartered Institute of Library and Information Professionals (CILIP) – carries lists of accredited courses and vacancies for graduate training positions. Tel: 020 7255 0500. www.cilip.org.uk

Chartered Institute of Library and Information Professionals (CILIP) (in Wales) – tel: 01970 622174. www.dis.aber.ac.uk/cilip_w

Researcher

Researchers are used by a variety of organisations from government departments to trade unions, from political parties to market research companies.

In government you would normally be working within a government department and handling external and internal research enquiries, which could come from colleagues, other government departments, academics, local councils, regional development agencies and members of the public. A lot of the work would be desk research in libraries or via the internet, but you would use a variety of other techniques including surveys.

You could also find yourself briefing, orally or in writing, senior colleagues and government ministers on the research evidence that you have found. On occasions you might have to present papers at conferences.

Social researchers focus particularly on social issues, such as poverty, housing and changing social attitudes. They may be employed by public bodies, trades unions, social research bodies and commercial firms, including market research agencies. After getting a brief from your client you might use a variety of research techniques. These could include desk research, quantitative and qualitative research, questionnaires and so on. With some agencies this could include developing and testing new theories.

There is also political research. Political researchers generally work for political parties or individual Members of Parliament (MPs) (where research may be one element of their role in assisting the MP). Apart from researching political issues in depth, you would monitor the media and Hansard (which reports parliamentary debates verbatim) to spot emerging political issues and to identify possible lines of attack that could be used against your party's rivals. You will also prepare briefs and policy papers as well as ghost write articles and speeches for your party's MPs.

Although political researchers are usually associated with the House of Commons, there are also opportunities working within the House of Lords, and for politicians in the European Parliament and devolved UK parliaments.

Entry qualifications

Although any degree is normally acceptable, for some areas of research, employers may prefer social science graduates.

Training and career development

Training tends to be on the job. Working as a political researcher is often used as a stepping stone towards becoming an MP or senior party official.

Finding vacancies

While at university, or if a recent graduate, you can access information about potential employers and current graduate vacancies through your university careers service. Further details about the services available through university careers services are provided in Chapter three.

Sources of further information

MRS (The Market Research Society) – tel: 020 7490 4911. www.mrs.org.uk

National Centre for Social Research – tel: 020 7250 1866. www.natcen.ac.uk

Office for National Statistics – tel: 0845 601 3034. www.ons.gov.uk

The Social Research Association – tel: 020 7388 2391. www.the-sra.org.uk

Chapter seventeen

Careers in management

In this chapter we'll look at the basic role of a manager and describe some of the management functions in which you could make a career:

- accounting and finance
- buying
- facilities management
- human resources (HR) or personnel management
- logistics
- management services and management consultancy
- marketing
- product development
- production
- sales.

A manager is responsible for running an organisation, a section of an organisation, or taking responsibility of a particular function across the organisation. Whether you are managing a manufacturing company, a business that provides a service or a government department, the principles are the same. You must develop products or services that satisfy your customers' needs while controlling costs, and ensure they are available when and where they are needed. As public service is covered in Chapter eighteen, this chapter concentrates on business organisations.

The traditional structure of management comprises line managers who head a section of a department or a whole department, who, in turn, report to senior managers who plan, coordinate and supervise the activities of all departments so that they work together effectively. At senior management level, the work involves making policy decisions, setting strategy and long-term planning. No two organisations are exactly the same in how they are structured – some have much 'flatter' hierachies (fewer levels of staff) than others.

In some organisations you will find project managers, who lead a team that has been created to undertake a specific job or project for a specific time period. One of the biggest differences of working in a project management role is that you may not have responsibility for a permanent team of your own staff.

However, most managers are concerned with long-term operational management. This involves implementing policy decisions and organising resources so that the activities of the business run smoothly and profitably. As an operational manager, you will typically:

- set your team's objectives and targets
- plan the work of the department or section
- attend planning and other meetings
- prepare budgets and get them agreed by senior management
- ensure you have the resources that your department needs and keep to agreed budgets
- keep records and monitor them against targets and budgets
- report progress to senior management
- train, develop, supervise and motivate your staff
- monitor the quality of the work done by your team
- monitor individual performance, making sure that targets are met
- keep your staff informed about what's going on within the organisation
- constantly seek better ways of doing things
- solve problems when they arise
- liaise with managers in other departments
- liaise with suppliers and customers, as appropriate.

Management functions

The following section outlines the main areas of business in which managers are employed.

Accounting and finance

Every business must keep full details of all its financial transactions and have them audited each year. To control the money going in and out of a business, each department works to a budget. Departmental managers need to know, monthly or even more often, how they are doing against their budgets through a system of 'management accounting'. **Management accountants** are employed within the organisation to collect and analyse the organisation's financial information in order to forecast results, create business plans, control budgets, prepare reports and so on. **Financial accountants** oversee the financial transactions of an organisation. This includes managing the payment of wages, taxes, invoices, preparing accounts, managing investments and carrying out internal audits.

The openings for graduates in finance are discussed in more detail in Chapter fourteen.

Buying

All organisations need to buy goods and materials to go about their business, and this is the role of the buyer. Manufacturers buy raw materials and components to make their products. This is not just a matter of negotiating a good price, but also of securing consistent quality and guaranteed delivery times.

Retailers buy goods for resale, either direct from manufacturers or from wholesalers. Retail buyers are concerned with recognising and predicting customer buying trends and finding the products to satisfy them. In service industries, buyers are responsible for acquiring all those supplies necessary for their business to operate – for instance, in hotels they might buy everything from buildings to bedding.

Facilities management

In larger organisations, facilities managers take responsibility for looking after the buildings and the services provided within them. They make sure that the buildings are well maintained, and organise services such as cleaning, security, air conditioning, heating and communications.

Facilities managers also have major responsibility if any moves to new premises are scheduled.

Human resources (HR)/Personnel management

A business must recruit, train and develop staff for every function. It must also care for everyone's health, safety and welfare, make sure that people are paid fairly, deal with equal opportunities and much more. This is the role of the HR or personnel manager. Many HR managers, particularly in large organisations, specialise in specific areas, such as recruitment or training.

Logistics

Logistics is concerned with making sure goods, materials or components are in the right place at the right time. For example, in manufacturing, after goods are made, they are traditionally stored until needed. Then, when required, they are distributed in such a way that they reach the customer on time and in perfect condition. Customers may be anywhere in the world. Controlling costs by careful route planning is vital. Reliability of delivery is also a responsibility of the logistics manager; goods and components often need to be delivered to a production line only a few hours before they are needed, or delivered to a supermarket and put on display. So late deliveries will do your business reputation no good at all!

Management services and management consultancy

Rather than managing an organisation or department directly, staff working in management services and management consultancy use specialist skills and expertise to find solutions to business problems, such as improving productivity.

There are many specialisms within **management services**. These include method study – observing how tasks are performed, before developing and putting in place new, more efficient ways of working; management control – making sure that organisations conform to relevant regulations; and information management – such as analysing information needs and implementing appropriate ICT systems.

Management consultants advise organisations how to manage their affairs more effectively. A management consultancy company may be brought in to solve a specific problem, to find ways to improve existing operations or to conduct feasibility studies. After investigation and analysis, management consultants will recommend actions to be taken.

Marketing

Marketing managers identify markets for existing and new products. They might suggest ideas for new products that need to be developed. They investigate potential new markets and existing markets to find out what new products could be introduced. The marketing team will either conduct or commission market research. Marketing managers work with specialists to create an identity or 'image' for the product through carefully thought out brand names, packaging, advertising and other promotional campaigns. Marketing managers need to be aware of what their competitors are doing and monitor the performance of products in terms of sales, customer satisfaction and profitability.

Product development

This concerns creating new or improved products. If you're in business to make such things as ready-made foods, pharmaceuticals, computers or toiletries, you will have research and development teams of scientists and technologists. If your products are items such as fabrics, furniture, clothing or jewellery then designers will create these. The production development team must liaise with marketing, in order to design products that meet customer needs, and with production, to ensure that the designs are practical to make.

Production

Products are made in many ways. These include computer-controlled production lines for making items such as cars, continuous process plants such as oil and chemical refineries, and assembly lines in which people build up parts into finished products. Or products may be 'one-offs' and made to order – from a specialist tooling machine to a cruise liner. It is the role of the production manager to ensure that the operations run as smoothly and as efficiently as possible. The job includes responsibility for staff, maintenance, planning the workload and, of course, dealing with any problems that are causing delays in manufacturing as quickly as possible.

Sales

Selling is about persuading people to buy your products. Sales managers call on potential and existing customers. They identify customer needs through discussion and then show how the company's product can satisfy that customer's needs better than those of its competitors.

Promotion could be to regional sales manager, looking after a team of sales staff. At head office, management staff in the sales department also take responsibility for making sure that new orders are processed efficiently, queries are dealt with and that any problems are resolved.

Entry qualifications

In most companies, it is possible for staff to work their way up into management positions, through a successful work track record and gaining qualifications through part-time study. Larger organisations also recruit graduates into trainee management posts. Any degree subject is normally acceptable, although for some specialist areas of management, a relevant degree may be required or preferred.

Work experience (from vacation work, work placements linked to your studies and so on) is especially valued. If you are attracted to working in business, it is worth remembering that foreign language skills could also be valuable.

Apart from the above, potential employers will be particularly interested in your personal qualities and skills. Managers need to be flexible, and able to constantly reprioritise their work, because problems can arise at any moment and must often be dealt with at once. So, if you like getting your head down to concentrate on one thing at a time without interruption, then management may not be for you! Managers must also be able to motivate those around them; effective managers earn the respect and cooperation of their team.

In addition, to be an effective manager you need to be self-confident, have the ability to build up good working relationships with others, and be able to communicate clearly and persuasively, orally and in writing. You need good problem-solving and organisational skills, and to be capable of working to deadlines and under pressure. You must be able to argue your point of view persuasively, and yet be willing to listen and learn, and make compromises when appropriate.

Training and career development

There are two usual entry routes into a management career – through a graduate management training scheme, usually run only by large organisations, and direct entry into a particular post.

Graduate management training programmes usually take around 18-24 months, and typically combine skills training and project work. You're likely to spend time in a number of functions. This will help you to understand how the business works as a whole, and to find out which specialist area is best suited to your interests and aptitudes.

After the training programme, you may be expected to study towards professional qualifications, such as those offered by the Chartered Management Institute or the Institute of Operations Management. If you are moving into a specialist area you may study towards the qualifications of the appropriate professional body, such as the Chartered Institute of Marketing, the Chartered Institute of Management Accountants or the Chartered Institute of Personnel and Development. You'll usually get day release and possibly some study leave before your examinations, and your employer will pay your fees and other expenses – but most of your study will be in your free time.

If you are a direct entrant, you will undergo 'induction training' to learn about the organisation, the goods or services it provides, its systems and so on. You will then start your job. Initially, you will work under close supervision – being trained on the job. You are likely to go on courses from time to time. Depending on your function, you may also be able to study part time for a relevant professional qualification. Whatever your entry route, as you become more senior you will become increasingly concerned with coordinating the activities of different functions, and so move into general management. You may consider gaining a masters degree in business administration (MBA).

Finding vacancies

Vacancies may be listed on employers' websites and in national and regional newspapers. While at university, or if a recent graduate, you can access information about potential employers and current graduate vacancies through your university careers service. Further details about the services available through university careers services are provided in Chapter three.

Sources of further information

Chartered Management Institute – tel: 01536 204222.
www.managers.org.uk

Institute of Leadership and Management – tel: 01543 266867.
www.i-l-m.com

Institute of Operations Management – tel: 01536 740105.
www.iomnet.org.uk

There are many chartered institutes and professional bodies representing all aspects of management; search online for those that are relevant to your particular interests.

Chapter eighteen

Careers in public service

There are two broad areas of public service in the UK – the Civil Service and local government. Further afield, there are the various institutions of the European Union. This chapter looks at all three career areas.

Civil Service

There are more than 170 government departments and agencies, employing nearly half a million people in the UK. Collectively, the Civil Service is Britain's largest employer of graduates. It is responsible for a huge range of services that affect almost every area of our lives – from education and employment to transport and the court services. Contrary to some assumptions, only one in five civil servants works in London.

Graduates may expect to join at executive officer level. At this level, you would normally be responsible for putting government policy into practice. You would look after the day-to-day operations in your particular area of work. Your duties may include:

- supervising a team
- producing reports
- giving presentations
- managing information
- liaising with people in other departments and agencies
- undertaking research
- dealing with members of the public.

At more senior levels, staff are responsible, under government ministers, for formulating and carrying out the policy of the government of the day. The focus of the work is on policy making. Activities can include:

- researching and analysing policy options
- consulting and negotiating with people in other organisations
- developing systems to implement policies
- drafting replies to Parliamentary questions
- drafting new laws
- supporting ministers in departmental management.

Entry qualifications

Graduates either enter the Civil Service through the recruitment schemes of the individual departments or agencies, or apply for the Fast Stream entry route.

Fast Stream recruitment is aimed at those with exceptional ability and the potential to progress quickly. The minimum entry requirement is a second class degree, in any subject, although some more specialised areas of government require particular degree subjects, such as science or a numerate subject. In the recruitment process, the selectors will be looking particularly at the skills and personal qualities applicants have to offer. These include excellent communication and leadership skills, the ability to develop good relationships, and to be able to think flexibly and handle pressure.

The Graduate Fast Stream is subdivided into five areas: central departments (i.e. major government departments other than the Foreign and Commonwealth Office); the Diplomatic Service; Houses of Parliament; European Fast Stream; and science and engineering.

There are also a few, more specialist Fast Stream schemes: the Economists Fast Stream, Statisticians Fast Stream, HR Fast Stream and Technology in Business (which focuses on IT). Details of these schemes and further information on the Graduate Fast Stream are found on the Fast Stream website, listed below.

For mainstream recruitment, there is a wide range of opportunities across all areas of government. Each department sets its own entry criteria. Often departments don't specify particular educational qualifications, as they select applicants against the competencies and skills required for the particular job.

For more information visit the Civil Service website or individual departmental websites listed below.

Training and career development

Most Fast Streamers begin their careers with a series of placements or 'postings' - different jobs within their departments. Each posting lasts around 12 or 18 months, after which entrants move on to another project or area of work. There are also secondment opportunities, which could include working in another government department, or in business or industry. Entrants also receive about 15 days formal training a year, and there may be the opportunity to gain professional qualifications through part-time study or distance learning. Eventually, Fast Streamers either work in researching and developing government policy, operational delivery of services to the public, or in corporate services, such as human resources or finance.

For staff at executive officer level, training is mostly on the job, although departments and agencies run management development training to improve the promotion prospects of suitable staff. You may be considered for specialist training if you show a particular aptitude. Once you have a year's service, you may apply for the in-service Fast Stream.

Finding vacancies

Civil Service vacancies are found on the websites listed below.

N.B. The NHS employs its own managers, separately from the civil servants in the Department of Health.

While at university, or if a recent graduate, you can access current graduate vacancies through your university careers service. Further details about the advice and information available through university careers services are provided in Chapter three.

Information about prison officers is included in Chapter nineteen.

Sources of further information

Civil Service Fast Stream Development Programme – tel: 01276 400333. www.civilservice.gov.uk/faststream

For vacancies across all departments – www.civilservice.gov.uk/jobs

Civil Service main departments and agencies include:

Crown Prosecution Service – brings criminals to trial. www.cps.gov.uk

Department for Business, Innovation & Skills – www.bis.gov.uk

Department for Culture, Media and Sports – www.culture.gov.uk

Department for Education – www.education.gov.uk

Department for Environment, Food and Rural Affairs – www.defra.gov.uk

Department of Health – www.dh.gov.uk

Department for International Development – provides overseas aid and assistance. www.dfid.gov.uk

Department for Transport – www.dft.gov.uk

Department for Work and Pensions – www.dwp.gov.uk

Foreign and Commonwealth Office – overseas relations. www.fco.gov.uk

GCHQ (Government Communications Headquarters) – www.gchq.gov.uk

Health and Safety Executive – www.hse.gov.uk

HM Revenue and Customs – assesses and collects taxes, excise duties, VAT, etc. www.hmrc.gov.uk

HM Treasury – public revenues/expenditure and the financial system. www.hm-treasury.gov.uk

Home Office – immigration and passports, drugs policy, counter-terrorism and the police. www.homeoffice.gov.uk

Ministry of Defence – www.mod.uk

Ministry of Justice – www.justice.gov.uk

Office for National Statistics – www.ons.gov.uk

NHS Graduate Management Training Scheme – www.nhsleadtheway.co.uk

Local government

Local government is concerned with providing services to the community. In career terms, it is a group of several hundred employers throughout the UK.

Services provided by local government authorities include:

- education
- environmental health
- fire and rescue service
- highways (building and repairs, traffic management, street lights, pavements, snow clearing)
- housing
- libraries
- police
- recreation, leisure, arts and museums
- social services
- strategic and local planning
- tourism promotion
- trading standards (consumer protection)
- transport
- waste and recycling services

- youth and community services, including, in England, the Connexions service, which provides careers guidance and personal support on a range of other issues to young people. (N.B. Connexions services may be provided directly by local government or contracted out – see Chapter twenty for information on working as a careers adviser.)

In some areas there are two levels (or 'tiers') of local government – county councils and district councils, and in other areas there are unitary (i.e. single tier) authorities. County councils provide the large-scale strategic services such as education and highways. Unitary authorities provide all local government services.

As you'll realise from looking at the list of services above, there's a huge range of career opportunities available. A number of these are professional careers. Many careers, such as accountancy and finance, archive work, IT, librarianship, museum work and public relations can be followed both inside and outside local government. For other career areas, such as the police, local government is the major or only employer.

Local government also employs many people in administrative roles, for example managers who hold senior departmental posts. They provide support to council committees and subcommittees, advise councillors, and research and prepare reports, sometimes involving the compilation and analysis of statistical information.

Entry qualifications

Specific entry qualifications vary depending on the position. Some may seek graduates from any discipline, while others of a more specialist nature require or prefer graduates with particular degree subjects.

For the National Graduate Development Programme (see below) you will need a 2:1 degree, in any discipline. The skills sought include the ability to work with others, good communication and persuasion skills, and planning and organisational skills.

Training and career development

Local authorities generally have a good reputation regarding their commitment to the training and development of their staff. Employees often study part time for work-related qualifications, including relevant professional qualifications.

The **National Graduate Development Programme**, run by the Improvement and Development Agency, is a fast-track route for graduates to train and prepare for senior management. It lasts for two years, and is based around a series of core placements within a host local council, supported by an external mentor and the Graduate Leadership Academy. The programme includes skills training and leads to a postgraduate diploma in local government management. You can find out more on: www.ngdp.co.uk.

Some councils run their own graduate training schemes. You can get information on these from their human resources departments. Schemes may be in particular occupational areas, such as finance, or may offer general management training.

Promotion opportunities at senior level may be restricted within a single authority. Career advancement is commonly made by moving from one local authority to another.

Finding vacancies

You can search current vacancies at the official local government jobs website www.LGjobs.com. Otherwise, you should look out for advertisements for specific vacancies. You will find these in *Opportunities: The Public Sector Recruitment Weekly* – see the website at www.opportunities.co.uk. You can also look in relevant professional and trade journals, and in national and local papers.

Recruitment into the National Graduate Development Programme, which recruits 80 trainees each year, is through www.ngdp.co.uk.

While at university, or if a recent graduate, you can access current graduate vacancies through your university careers service. Further details about the advice and information available through university careers services are provided in Chapter three.

Sources of further information

www.LGtalent.com – carries information on the range of career opportunities within local government.

The European institutions

The European Commission and other institutions of the European Union (EU) are having an ever-increasing impact on life in the UK and other member countries.

The main European institutions are:

- **The European Commission** – develops legislation; ensures legislation is implemented; represents the community internationally

- **The Council of the European Union** – composed of ministers from each member state; the EU's main decision-making and coordinating body

- **The European Parliament** – approves or amends proposed legislation; has the last word on aspects of the budget

- **The European Court of Justice** – rules on the interpretation and application of EU law

- **The European Court of Auditors** – supervises the EU's budget

- **The European Ombudsman** – deals with complaints against EU institutions and bodies

- **The European Economic and Social Committee** and the **Committee of the Regions** – represent employers and employees, and local and regional bodies.

The European Commission is the largest institution, offering the most employment opportunities. Staff help formulate legislation, develop policies and oversee their day-to-day implementation. Graduates are generally recruited into administrator (AD) grades.

Administrators work in many areas including administration, law, finance, economics, communication and science. Day-to-day work may involve formulating legislation, developing and implementing policies, analysing and advising, coordinating economic and other policies, taking part in trade negotiations, or representing their institution in international meetings.

Entry qualifications

You need to be an EU citizen. All staff need to have a very good working knowledge of at least one other official EU language besides their own. People interested in a career in the EU should also have an enthusiasm for working in the EU, strong interpersonal skills and an awareness of current affairs. To be recruited into the AD grades, you need a degree. Some posts may have specific requirements about degree subject and class. Relevant work experience may be required.

You can prepare yourself for working in the EU through applying initially for the European Fast Stream of the UK Civil Service, as described earlier in this chapter. Apart from at least a second class honours degree, you must have A level French or German at grades A*-C, or equivalent. For the first two years, you will be given EU-related postings in the Civil Service, receive further language training and undertake a six-month work placement in the European Commission. You will then be expected to enter all the EU competitions (the recruitment process for EU vacancies) for which you are eligible.

Training and career development

Further language training is available to those who are appointed. There is a well-defined career structure. The AD grade consists of levels 5 to 16. New entrants start at level 5, and good performance leads to promotion to a higher level. Most people spend three to six years at each level.

Finding vacancies

Recruitment is undertaken by a system called 'open competition'. There are several stages to the recruitment process, taking several months. While each institution is responsible for its own recruitment, joint recruitment competitions are held.

Competitions are advertised in the national press and the *Official Journal of the European Union* (available online). There's also a centralised recruitment website for all EU institutions, which is operated by the European Personnel Selection Office (EPSO) - listed below.

Sources of further information

The European Commission Representation in the UK - tel: 020 7973 1992. www.ec.europa.eu/unitedkingdom

European Personnel Selection Office (EPSO) - the centralised recruitment website for all EU institutions (for information on traineeships, having selected the English option, click on 'Discover EU careers' then 'EU careers' and finally 'staff categories'). www.europa.eu/epso

UK Office of the European Parliament - tel: 020 7227 4300. www.europarl.org.uk

Chapter nineteen

Careers in the uniformed services

The main uniformed professions that recruit graduates are the:

- Armed Forces (the Army, Royal Air Force, Royal Navy and Royal Marines)
- police
- prison service.

Although they cover a range of very different activities, they have some things in common:

- they provide a public service, often in dangerous or distressing situations
- there's a lot of discipline – obeying orders is a fundamental aspect of the work, but self-discipline is also important
- they may be in a position of authority over others
- they work unsocial hours.

The nature of the work, the shared risks, the discipline and the irregular hours tend to give the uniformed services a distinct identity and a strong sense of camaraderie.

Armed Forces officer

The main purpose of the Armed Forces is to defend our country – the world is rarely free from conflict and there are constant threats from terrorism, but their work also extends to peacekeeping missions and disaster relief. Servicemen and women must be prepared to risk their lives at any time, whatever the scenario. As well as considering whether you are prepared to take this risk, you also need to face the moral question – would you be prepared to kill or order the killing of others?

If you decide the way of life, and all that it entails, is for you, the Armed Forces offer a huge range of career opportunities. Most officers in the Armed Forces have two roles: to lead and manage a team of people, and to be a technical specialist. The balance between the two roles varies by rank and by the service you're in. While it is not necessary to be a graduate to become an officer in the Armed Forces, there are plenty of officer positions for graduates of any discipline.

Each of the Armed Forces operates along broadly similar lines, with personnel typically specialising in one of the following areas:

- **combat** – for example, as officers of the infantry, artillery and armoured regiments of the Army; as warfare officers in the Royal Navy, who command ships and submarines; as pilots and weapon systems officers of the Royal Air Force (RAF) who fly fast jets and helicopters; and as commando officers in the Royal Marines

- **operational support** – the Army Air Corps, for example, carries troops to where they are needed, performs reconnaissance missions and provides airborne command posts; while the Royal Navy and RAF also offer support roles, such as air traffic controllers and aerospace battle managers

- **engineering** – military engineering during combat operations may include mine clearing, the demolition of key targets with explosives, and post-conflict reconstruction and humanitarian support; on an ongoing basis, engineers maintain, fit and test the full range of military equipment from ships' engines to rocket launchers

- **logistics** – officers working in logistics ensure that the necessary people, equipment and supplies are where they are needed at any given time – at home or on operations

- **intelligence** – involves the collection, analysis and presentation of information about the enemy and aims to combat espionage, subversion and sabotage

- **medical services** – whether in field hospitals or at home, Armed Forces personnel need access to healthcare specialists, such as nurses and doctors

- **signals/communications** – involves the maintenance and operation of the various command, control and information systems, as well as providing secure communication worldwide

- **administrative support** – a huge amount of administration is required to run organisations the size and complexity of the Armed Forces; opportunities exist in education and training services, personnel management, public relations, accountancy, legal services, estate management and so on.

Entry qualifications

In general, any degree subject is accepted – although certain regiments and corps may prefer a particular degree, depending on their needs. (Professionally-qualified officers, however, need to hold professional qualifications in their chosen field, for example law or medicine, before applying for officer training.) For some roles, language skills are an asset.

As well as your degree, personal qualities are important. Armed Forces recruiters look for applicants who are assertive and good problem solvers, and who have plenty of common sense and initiative. The ability to make quick decisions based on sound judgement is important, as is the ability to express yourself easily and clearly. Obviously, you need to be physically fit and have plenty of stamina, and, perhaps most crucially as an officer, you need leadership skills and the ability to motivate others by your personal example.

Officer recruitment takes place via selection boards. These combine interviews, tests and leadership tasks; these assessment sessions last several days. Procedures vary a little from service to service, but are always rigorous and demanding. The individual boards are:

- the Army Officer Selection Board - for the Army

- the Admiralty Interview Board - for the Royal Navy

- the Officers and Aircrew Selection Centre - for the RAF.

Training and career development

For any of the Armed Forces, initial officer training aims to develop your leadership skills, your understanding of the military and the specialist skills required for your particular role. It is designed to be challenging both physically and mentally, and requires your total commitment. Initial training typically lasts between six to twelve months; however, training will be ongoing throughout your career as required. You will learn a range of skills that are directly transferable to a management career in civilian life. Employers generally welcome people with service experience because of their self-discipline and leadership qualities.

On joining the Armed Forces you will be required to sign up to a minimum period of engagement, the shortest period is around three to four years, although it may be longer where lengthy training is involved. Promotion is usually automatic in the early stages. Promotion to the very highest ranks, though, is by competition and is awarded on merit.

Finding vacancies

Your local Armed Forces Careers Office (AFCO) can give you detailed information about specific jobs, how to apply, the terms of your commission and so on. They also arrange interviews and tests.

If you are still at school you should contact the AFCO to find out more about the scholarships and bursaries available to students during their last two years (aged 16 to 18) at school or college. There are also schemes to sponsor those who wish to become officers through their university course. You should apply as soon as you have a confirmed university place or as soon as possible on starting your degree course.

While at university, or as a recent graduate, you can access information about graduate opportunities in the Armed Forces through your university careers service. Further information about the services available through university careers services is provided in Chapter three.

Sources of further information

You can get more details and copies of up-to-date literature on graduate careers from your local AFCO.

Army careers - tel: 0845 7300111. www.army.mod.uk

RAF careers - tel: 0845 605 555. www.raf.mod.uk/careers

Royal Navy and Royal Marines careers - tel: 0845 600 1444. www. royalnavy.mod.uk and www.royalnavy.mod.uk/marines

Police officer

The UK does not have a national police force, but 43 separate forces in England and Wales, eight in Scotland and one in Northern Ireland. Their role is to protect life and property, and to enforce law and order. When a crime has been committed, police officers provide help to the victims and witnesses, while using a range of traditional and highly sophisticated methods of investigation to identify and apprehend offenders.

All entrants start work as uniformed constables on the beat. The work includes helping members of the public and answering queries, checking the security of premises, apprehending and interviewing suspects, investigating crimes and taking statements from witnesses, and dealing with accidents, disturbances and traffic problems. Not all their time is spent on foot or car patrol. There's a lot of paperwork and some time is spent in court.

Later, you can specialise in areas such as:

- the CID (Criminal Investigation Department), which investigates serious crimes

- the traffic department, which promotes road safety, controls traffic flow, and deals with traffic accidents and offences

- the river police service, which patrols rivers and coastal waters to prevent theft and smuggling, and performs life saving

- a firearms unit, an option for experienced officers who need to pass rigorous and frequent training courses to work as police marksmen.

Entry qualifications

You need to be physically fit and in good health; there are also minimum eyesight standards that apply. Candidates must pass background and security checks, among other criteria regarding eligibility. As a graduate, you could consider the High Potential Development Scheme (HPDS) as a fast-track route to senior leadership positions within the police. Although the scheme is also open to non-graduates, it involves a high level of academic study and a workplace-related dissertation, leading to a postgraduate diploma in police leadership. The highest performers can ultimately undertake a development programme leading to a masters qualification.

The HPDS selection procedure has several stages and includes ability tests, interviews, individual aptitude tests and group exercises. To be accepted onto the HPDS, you need to demonstrate a range of skills in the areas of communication, problem solving, planning and organisation, community focus, respect for race and diversity, strategic thinking and openness to change.

Training and career development

All new recruits undergo a two-year training period called the Initial Police Learning and Development Programme (IPLDP). The training is designed to give student police officers the skills, knowledge and understanding that they will need to do their jobs effectively. The programmes involves on-the-job and classroom-based learning about the community you serve, your local force and its procedures, health and safety, the law, crime prevention and so on. You will undertake placements with different departments within your force, before starting patrol work.

Promotion is through the ranks, from constable through to sergeant, then inspector – at which level your time is divided between operational and management duties. At any rank, you can apply for transfer to another force, and experience in other forces is essential for the more senior postings. The more senior you become, the more you will be involved in liaising with the leaders of the community you serve. Unlike other police officers, those on the HPDS do not have to wait for a vacancy to become available in order to apply for a promotion. Instead they may be promoted by their chief officer as soon as they demonstrate their suitability for the next rank.

Finding vacancies

Vacancies are advertised on the 'Police Could You?' website, listed below. You can only apply for the HPDS after being recruited as a police officer. Some people work first as special constables or police community support officers as a way of gaining experience, before applying to become a police officer.

While at university, or as a recent graduate, you can access information about vacancies with the police through your university careers service. Further information about the help available through university careers services is provided in Chapter three.

Sources of further information

The National Policing Improvement Agency – for general enquiries about the HPDS. Tel: 020 7021 7070. www.npia.police.uk/hpds

www.policecouldyou.co.uk – for information about the work of the police, plus a list of UK police forces (except Scotland) and their vacancies.

Prison officer

HM Prison Service is entrusted with protecting the public by holding prisoners securely and reducing the risk of them re-offending. In doing so, it aims to care for prisoners in safe and well-ordered establishments; there are about 130 institutions in England and Wales. As well as convicted offenders of all ages who have been sentenced to various terms of imprisonment, there are also remand prisoners awaiting either trial or sentencing by the courts.

The main duty of prison officers is to maintain security and control within a prison: supervising the prisoners in all areas, including during exercise and free time, mealtimes and while they are in their cells. They also receive new prisoners and complete the necessary paperwork. They pass on to senior staff any requests that prisoners may have.

A major role for prison officers is the rehabilitation of convicted offenders. They have daily contact with the prisoners and get to know them well. Officers make sure that individuals get professional help when they need it, and generally prepare them for making the right choices in life outside the prison. For this aspect of their work, prison officers need well-developed communication skills – in order to listen to, influence and help offenders. The ability to form relationships with a diverse range of people is important – some prisoners can be extremely difficult and potentially violent, while others are at risk from suicide or self-harm.

Entry qualifications

For general entry to the service there are no specific academic requirements, but the National Offender Management Scheme (NOMS) offers a programme aimed exclusively at graduates who are either predicted, or who have gained, a 2:1 degree in any subject. The selection process includes ability tests, role-play exercises, written tests and an interview.

Applicants to the scheme need to believe in the value of rehabilitation and be able to demonstrate the skills needed to eventually take on senior leadership roles within the prison service. For example, you need to be decisive – yet fair and calm, even in volatile situations. Self-confidence is also important – you can't be intimidated by individuals or events, and if you do face problems, you need the resilience to persevere.

The Prison Service also directly recruits into a wide range of functions suitable for graduates, including forensic psychology, finance, procurement, human resources and healthcare.

Training and career development

The NOMS Graduate Programme lasts three years and begins with a six-week course at the national training centre in Rugby. Here you learn the basic duties of a prison officer, such as applying control and restraint techniques, using handcuffs and conducting searches. The final week of the course is spent shadowing a prison officer at work, after which you will be given your first post. By the third year of the programme, you will be expected to take on managerial responsibilities – perhaps as an operational manager or on a secondment with the Ministry of Justice. At the end of the graduate programme, you will need to gain a broad range of experience (of different risk categories; of male, female and juvenile prisoners; and of the different functions of the prison service) before you can take on a position as a deputy governor or governor of your own prison.

Finding vacancies

Recruitment drives for the NOMS Graduate Programme operate on an annual basis; full details are available on the HM Prison Service website listed below. Check with HM Prison Service for the deadline for applications, or sign up for 'job alerts' via their website.

While at university, or as a recent graduate, you can access information about graduate vacancies available with HM Prison Service through your university careers service. Further information about the help available through university careers services is provided in Chapter three.

Sources of further information

HM Prison Service – tel: 020 7217 600. www.hmprisonservice.gov.uk

Chapter twenty

Other options

It would be impossible to list all possible careers that are open to you – if you refer back to Chapter five, you will see that graduate destinations are many and varied! With some research, and perhaps some advice and guidance from a professional careers adviser, you may be able to identify many more careers that would suit your situation.

This chapter covers just a few more options you may like to consider, in the areas of:

- careers guidance
- housing
- ICT
- legal work
- retailing
- surveying.

Finally, you might like to give a thought to self-employment, which, if you have a commercially-viable idea and the skills to deliver it, can be a tempting proposition! Information about self-employment is provided at the end of this chapter.

Careers guidance

Careers guidance specialists, or careers advisers, help people of all ages make decisions about their education, training and future career. Their role is not to tell people what to do, but instead to help their clients come to a better understanding of their options and help them plan how to achieve their goals, based on their individual abilities, preferences and priorities.

The work involves one-to-one interviews with clients; group sessions; advising other professionals, such as teachers; report writing and record keeping. Careers advisers may help organise careers events in association with employers, training providers and educational institutions – and must keep up to date with local and national issues relating to careers. In some settings the work may involve liaising with potential employers and helping people find work or work experience.

Careers advisers may be employed within the government-funded Connexions and nextstep services (in England) or in Careers Services (in Wales, Scotland and Northern Ireland). They may also be directly employed by schools, colleges and universities. Other employers include private agencies and, occasionally, professional organisations, major employers and voluntary organisations.

N.B. There are plans to replace the nextstep service with a new 'adult advancement and careers service' in England, during 2010.

Entry qualifications

Specific entry requirements vary, but the most widely accepted professional careers qualification is the Qualification in Careers Guidance (QCG), which takes one year, full time, or two years, part time. It is open to graduates of any subject, and involves postgraduate-level study at a university combined with work-based learning. Alternatively, there are masters degrees in careers guidance and related subjects. It is also possible to qualify if you are already in relevant employment and have gained experience of working in guidance, by undertaking training leading to the NVQ level 4 in advice and guidance.

You need to have a real interest in people and be able to establish relationships quickly. Communication and listening skills are vital and you must be non-judgemental and patient. You will also need to be effective in using a wide range of paper-based and computerised information sources.

Training and career development

Advisers wishing to work in the Connexions service must complete additional training leading to specific units of the NVQ level 4 in learning, development and support services (LDSS) for children, young people and those who care for them. Connexions personal advisers (PAs) not only give guidance on careers, but also on a range of other issues relevant to young people such as housing, benefits, health issues, drugs and relationships.

Careers advisers and PAs undertake continuing professional development (CPD) throughout their careers. It is possible to specialise in working with different client groups, such as young people or adults, people with special needs, people in higher education, etc. With experience there are opportunities to take on supervisory or management positions, or to work on a self-employed basis as a careers consultant.

Finding vacancies

Jobs are advertised in *Portico* – a fortnightly vacancy bulletin published by the Institute of Career Guidance (ICG), in *The Guardian*, *The Independent* and *Times Higher Education*. Both the ICG and the Association of Graduate Careers Advisory Services (AGCAS) list vacancies on their websites.

While at university, or as a recent graduate, you can access information about potential employers and current graduate vacancies through your university careers service. Further information about the help available through university careers services is provided in Chapter three.

Sources of further information

Association of Graduate Careers Advisory Services (AGCAS) – tel: 0114 251 5750. www.agcas.org.uk

Institute of Career Guidance (ICG) – tel: 01384 376464. www.icg-uk.org

Housing

People working in housing are responsible for the planning, construction, allocation and upkeep of rented properties. Many jobs are concerned with creating and maintaining sustainable communities (places where people want to live and work, now and in the future). Graduates with a degree in any subject may find vacancies as a trainee housing manager. You are likely to be given experience of a wide range of responsibilities before, possibly, specialising in one area. You may get involved in planning housing requirements; purchasing land; commissioning new builds; managing lettings, transfers and exchanges; overseeing repairs and maintenance; and working with other agencies to maintain good community relations.

The major employers are housing associations and local government bodies, such as district councils. The role of the local authority housing department is to make sure that the housing needs of their area are met. That includes making land available for building. Increasingly, responsibility for the management and the provision of new housing has moved to housing associations. Large private estates, cooperatives, charities and property-owning companies may also employ housing managers or property managers. The Armed Forces employ housing managers drawn from the ranks of serving officers.

Entry qualifications

You may be competing with people who have degrees in subjects more relevant to this career area; however, jobs are usually available to graduates of any subject and employers may be more concerned about the personal qualities and interests of potential employees. Postgraduate qualifications in subjects such as housing studies or sustainable communities may be useful.

You will need good communication and presentation skills. Commercial awareness and negotiation skills are also important. The work can be pressurised and you may need to develop a thorough understanding of relevant legislation, government policy and building construction.

Training and career development

Once in employment, there are opportunities to take relevant qualifications through part-time study or distance learning, including those offered by the Chartered Institute of Housing (CIH). Many people working in housing become members of the CIH. For information on membership grades and the requirements for each level, contact the CIH or see their website – listed at the end of this section.

Finding vacancies

The weekly magazine, *Inside Housing* (and its associated website), lists job vacancies in social housing. For vacancies within local government, visit www.LGtalent.com. Vacancies are also advertised by recruitment agencies, on many specialist and general online job sites, in the appointments sections of certain daily newspapers (particularly the society section of *The Guardian*, published every Wednesday) and on employers' own websites.

The National Housing Federation publishes a list of around 1,200 housing associations in its *Directory of Members*, which may be useful in finding employers in a particular area. The directory may be available for reference in your local library, or visit www.nhfdirectory.co.uk.

While at university, or as a recent graduate, you can access information about potential employers and current graduate vacancies through your university careers service. Further information about the help available through university careers services is provided in Chapter three.

Sources of further information

Asset Skills – the Sector Skills Council covering the housing sector. Tel: 0800 056 7160. www.assetskills.org

Chartered Institute of Housing (CIH) – tel: 024 7685 1700. www.cih.org

Institute of Residential Property Management – tel: 020 7622 5092. www.irpm.org.uk

National Housing Federation – tel: 020 7067 1010. www.housing.org.uk and www.nhfdirectory.co.uk

ICT

Computers are used in every type of workplace you can think of and, while you need a relevant degree to work in the more technical roles, there are many opportunities that are open to graduates of any discipline.

For example, **systems analysts and designers** first investigate and analyse a business problem, such as introducing a new booking system for hospital appointments or a complex payroll system, before identifying, costing and assessing potential ICT solutions. The work also involves project management – overseeing budgets, schedules and the work involved in implementing the new system.

Software may need to be developed or adapted to meet the business requirements and this is where people with programming skills come in. **Software developers** may specialise in different types of programming, such as website or back-end development. The work involves specifying what functionality the programme needs before writing and testing the code.

Database managers take responsibility for maintaining and developing an organisation's databases, which may store information about customers, accounts, orders, stock levels, etc. **ICT or systems managers** may have overall responsibility for the way ICT is used within an organisation, setting its policies and developing its long-term vision.

Entry qualifications

You may be competing with people who have degrees in subjects more relevant to this career area; however, employers often use aptitude tests to assess an applicant's suitability, and then provide specialist training. Postgraduate conversion courses in computing and ICT are available for graduates with unrelated degrees.

You need a logical mind as well as analytical and problem-solving skills for this type of work. The ability to work well in a team and communicate complex ideas to non-specialists is also important.

Training and career development

Training may be in-house or you may be able to work towards professional qualifications through part-time study or distance learning. Relevant qualifications are offered by the BCS (The Chartered Institute for IT), the Institute for the Management of Information Systems and some larger computer companies, such as Microsoft.

Finding vacancies

Vacancies are advertised by specialist recruitment agencies, on many specialist and general online job sites, in the appointments sections of certain daily newspapers and on employers' own websites.

While at university, or as a recent graduate, you can access information about potential employers and current graduate vacancies through your university careers service. Further information about the help available through university careers services is provided in Chapter three.

Sources of further information

BCS: The Chartered Institute for IT – tel: 0845 300 4417. www.bcs.org

e-skills UK – the Sector Skills Council for business and information technology. www.e-skills.com

Institute for the Management of Information Systems – tel: 0700 00 23456. www.imis.org.uk

Institution of Analysts and Programmers – tel: 020 8567 2118. www.iap.org.uk

The Institution of Engineering and Technology (IET) – tel: 01438 313311. www.theiet.org

Women in Technology – an organisation that aims to increase the number of women working as IT professionals and to help them build successful careers. www.womenintechnology.co.uk

Legal work

Barristers work in the courts defending and prosecuting cases referred to them by solicitors. They may also represent clients at public enquiries. Some barristers work as legal advisers and consultants. Queen's Counsels (QCs) and judges are selected from the ranks of barristers. Most barristers are self-employed, and work in chambers (offices). There are also employed opportunities, working for the Crown Prosecution Service and in the Government Legal Service.

Solicitors have day-to-day contact with the public, giving advice on all kinds of legal matters. They represent clients in the county courts and magistrates' courts (and, in certain circumstances, in the higher courts). Solicitors give instructions to barristers for the cases that barristers present in court. Solicitors usually specialise in areas such as property sale and purchase, company law, family law or criminal law. Solicitors work in private practice, commerce and industry, and for local government and the Civil Service, including the Crown Prosecution Service and the Government Legal Service.

Entry qualifications

Graduates of any subject can train to become barristers or solicitors. You need at least a second-class degree for entry to a conversion course; some employers may require at least a 2:1.

In addition, you also need a high level of intellect and ability to take in and assess large amounts of information. Self-confidence is required along with well-developed presentation and communication skills. You will need to be able to relate to a wide range of people and have the mental and physical stamina to deal with often long and complex cases.

Training and career development

To become a barrister or solicitor, non-law graduates must take a one-year, full-time (or two-year, part-time) conversion course – either the Common Professional Examination or an approved Graduate Diploma in Law.

Would-be barristers follow this by taking the Bar Professional Training Course (BPTC) – one year, full time or two years, part time. From September 2010, nine institutions will offer BPTCs; course fees cost around £14,000, although a limited number of grants and scholarships are available. During the BPTC, you develop practical skills in, for example, casework, negotiation and research. The next stage is to undertake a year's pupillage with an experienced barrister. After that, you apply for a tenancy in a set of chambers or for an employed position. Competition is stiff at all stages of the training.

To train as a solicitor, non-law graduates must take a conversion course, as described above. This must be followed by the Legal Practice Course (one year, full time or two years, part time – some more flexible routes are also available) and finally, you must find a two-year training contract in a solicitor's office or other approved organisation, during which you take a professional skills course. There is a great deal of competition for training contract positions.

Finding vacancies

Useful information about how to take your first steps into law can be found on www.lawcareers.net – published in association with the Law Society.

Sources of further information

The Bar Council – tel: 020 7242 0082. www.barcouncil.org.uk

Bar Standards Board – tel: 020 7611 1444. www.barstandardsboard.org.uk

Government Legal Service – tel: 0845 3000 793. www.gls.gov.uk

The Law Society – tel: 020 7242 1222. www.lawsociety.org.uk

Solicitors Regulation Authority – tel: 0870 606 2555. www.sra.org.uk

www.lawcareers.net – provides information about careers and training, as well as advertising vacancies for training posts and permanent positions.

Retailing

Large retailers offer many graduate opportunities in a variety of jobs such as finance, quality assurance, marketing, buying, merchandising and IT. Some of these functions are described in Chapter seventeen. However, the majority of openings are in **store management**.

Most vacancies are in supermarkets, multiples (chain stores specialising in areas such as electrical goods, books, outdoor sports, furniture and fashion) and department stores. Retail management may involve being in charge of a department – being responsible for staff, meeting sales targets, merchandising, dealing with customer complaints, health and safety, and security; or working as a branch manager – with similar responsibilities, but also involved in recruitment and training, organising sales promotions, stock control and so on.

Depending on the type of store you work for, you may be expected to work shifts, for example, some supermarkets are open 24 hours a day.

Entry qualifications

Graduate management training schemes usually accept any degree subject. It can be useful to be able to demonstrate relevant work experience and a good knowledge of the particular company that you wish to work for.

Training and career development

Training programmes tend to combine formal training with experience in different sections of the business, e.g. finance, HR and merchandising. This may involve travelling to, or working in, other parts of the country.

Finding vacancies

Vacancies are advertised on the websites of the major retailers and on many specialist and general online job sites. A useful website for vacancies, which includes a section for graduates, can be found at www.inretail.co.uk.

While at university, or as a recent graduate, you can access information about potential employers and current graduate vacancies through your university careers service. Further information about the help available through university careers services is provided in Chapter three.

Sources of further information

Skillsmart Retail – the Sector Skills Council for retail. Tel: 020 7462 5060. www.skillsmartretail.com

Surveying

Surveying covers a range of different career options, all involved with the measurement, valuation, management and development of property or resources. Depending on the branch, surveyors may advise on issues ranging from the environment or disabled access to buildings through to rural conservation or the restoration of historic buildings. They may value land and buildings, livestock, antiques and fine art. They may measure and record features for map-making or advise on mining projects or marine resources. The main branches of surveying are:

- general practice
- quantity surveying
- building surveying
- rural property surveying
- geomatic surveying
- planning and development surveyors
- marine resource management
- minerals and environmental surveying.

More detailed information on the work of a land (or geometrics) surveyor can be found in Chapter nine.

Entry qualifications

The Royal Institution of Chartered Surveyors (RICS) is the principal body representing surveyors. Other professional bodies also cover careers in surveying. As a graduate, to qualify as a chartered surveyor with RICS, you can begin by taking a RICS-accredited postgraduate qualification, open to graduates with a degree in any subject.

There are a number of other professional bodies related to surveying, each with their own entry requirements. Which body you choose can depend on a variety of factors, including the branch of surveying in which you intend to specialise.

You will need practical problem-solving skills, as well as an analytical and logical approach to your work. Good communication and teamworking skills are also important.

Training and career development

To achieve chartered status with RICS, you must complete a period of structured training in employment before undertaking the Assessment of Professional Competence (APC). Once fully qualified it is possible to be promoted to a senior management position or to work on a self-employed basis in private practice.

Finding vacancies

Vacancies are advertised on the websites of relevant professional bodies, including a dedicated job site run by RICS, www.ricsrecruit.com. Specialist recruitment agencies, as well as specialist and general online job sites, employers' own websites and certain daily newspapers, all carry vacancies for surveyors.

While at university, or as a recent graduate, you can access information about potential employers and current graduate vacancies through your university careers service. Further information about the help available though university careers services is provided in Chapter three.

Sources of further information

The Chartered Institute of Building – tel: 01344 630700. www.ciob.org.uk

Chartered Institution of Civil Engineering Surveyors – tel: 0161 972 3100. www.ices.org.uk

Chartered Surveyors Training Trust – tel: 020 7785 3850. www.cstt.org.uk

ConstructionSkills – the Sector Skills Council for the construction industry. Tel: 0844 844 0046. www.bconstructive.co.uk

Royal Institution of Chartered Surveyors (RICS) – tel: 0870 333 1600. www.rics.org/careers

Self-employment

Almost four million people in the UK are self-employed, a figure that includes people who run their own businesses in the usual sense, as well as those who work freelance for different employers. Opportunities for self-employment vary considerably, depending on your knowledge, skills and interests. Many arts and humanities graduates, particularly from the performing and visual arts – from singers and dancers to artists and photographers – are self-employed and work on a freelance basis.

Graduates who have qualified in a profession such as accountancy, law and so on can consider becoming self-employed and running their own practice. Others with management skills, for example, could potentially work as consultants or interim managers (for example, covering for the long-term absence of another manager). If you are enterprising and wish to go into business, then it will be down to you to research your market, devise a business plan and seek any necessary finance. Franchise opportunities allow you to buy into an established brand, although can still require large amounts of investment capital.

Entry qualifications

The most important requirements for self-employment relate to your personal drive, ambition and commercial awareness. You will need motivation and determination to succeed, and confidence and flexibility to do a wide range of tasks in support of your business. Skills in planning and organisation are also critical. You will also need a good understanding of the rules and regulations that apply to your type of business – including VAT, insurance, health and safety, data protection, etc.

Training and career development

You could consider taking courses in business, marketing, bookkeeping, IT and management. Many such courses are available on a distance-learning or part-time basis. There are several different agencies and organisations that offer advice, workshops, networking opportunities, mentoring, and so on to people who are considering self-employment. See below for further details.

Finding opportunities

While at university, or as a recent graduate, you should be able to access information about self-employment through your university careers service. Further information about the help available through university careers services is provided in Chapter three.

Sources of further information

British Franchise Association – tel: 01865 379892. www.thebfa.org

Business Link – a service operating across England, supported by government departments, agencies and local authorities, which advises new small- and medium-size businesses. Tel: 0845 600 9 006. www.businesslink.gov.uk

Co-operatives UK – tel: 0161 246 2900. www.cooperatives-uk.coop

Enterprise UK – an organisation run in partnership between the Department for Business, Innovation and Skills; British Chamber of Commerce; Confederation of British Industry; Federation of Small Businesses; and Institute of Directors. Tel: 020 7430 8010. www.enterpriseuk.org

Federation of Small Businesses – tel: 01253 336000. www.fsb.org.uk

Flexible Support for Business – a service provided by the Welsh Assembly Government that offers support and advice for businesses in Wales. Tel: 0300 060 3000. http://fs4b.wales.gov.uk

www.hmrc.gov.uk/selfemployed – HM Revenue & Customs.

www.shell-livewire.org – offers free online advice and support for anyone who is considering starting a business.

www.venturenavigator.co.uk – an online service, funded by the Government and created by a consortium of seven universities, which allows people with a business start-up idea to assess the viability of their idea, access relevant guidance and network with others.

Section 4
Other sources of information and advice

Chapter twenty-one

Other sources of information and advice

This chapter lists books and websites that may be helpful to you in choosing a degree course and university, finding information on specific careers, and graduate recruitment and postgraduate study. Many of them can be found in your school/college careers library or university careers advisory service, in your public library or by accessing the relevant websites. Otherwise, you could order and buy books through a good bookshop, online or from the publisher.

General

Student Life: a Survival Guide published by Lifetime Publishing, £11.99. A survival guide for anyone beginning, or soon to begin, university or college.

Decisions at 17/18+ published by Lifetime Publishing, £11.99. A student helpbook looking at the full range of choices at 18 – higher education and employment.

Degree course and university choice

University and College Entrance: The Official Guide (annual) published by the Universities and Colleges Admissions Service (UCAS), £31.50 (book and CD-ROM) or £15 (CD-ROM only). The 'Big Guide' provides details of all UK higher education courses at publicly-funded institutions.

University Degree Course Offers published by Trotman, £32.99. Lists all first degree courses, detailing grade and points requirements, gives advice on admissions tests and interviews, and profiles universities and colleges.

Choosing Your Degree Course and University published by Trotman, £22.99. Practical advice on how to select the right course and university; includes data on the relative quality of courses.

Which University? published by Trotman, £14.99. Includes tables that rate universities on everything from the quality of teaching to the make-up of the student population.

The Times Good University Guide 2010 published online at www.timesonline.co.uk profiles each UK university with league tables showing the strengths and weaknesses of each. You can search the interactive tables online by institution or subject and compare universities by a range of criteria.

How to Complete Your UCAS Application published by Trotman, £12.99. This useful volume helps you to apply for courses through UCAS. It takes you through the whole application process, giving all the essential dos and don'ts, as well as providing guidance on the very important 'personal statement'.

'Course Discover' – you might also want to consult this online resource. Working in partnership with over 1,000 UK and Irish universities and colleges, this lists more than 110,000 courses and gives details of course content, entry requirements, accommodation costs, disabled facilities, open-day dates and much more. If your school subscribes to this subscription-only service, you can consult it at home as well as at school. The website is at www.coursediscover.co.uk.

Careers

If you are not yet sure which career area interests you most, several books describe a wide range of careers with their entry requirements, training, etc. For example:

Careers 2010 published by Trotman, £45.00.

The Times A–Z of Careers and Jobs published by Kogan Page, £14.99.

The Penguin Careers Guide published by Penguin, £16.99.

Jobs and Careers after A levels published by Lifetime Publishing, £11.99.

The 'jobs4u' careers database at www.connexions-direct.com/jobs4u gives excellent information on jobs and careers. It covers virtually every type of job (manual to professional) with a description of the work, work environment, entry requirements, training, prospects, and pay and conditions.

'Explore types of jobs' at www.prospects.ac.uk is a very useful resource provided by Prospects. This provides up-to-date and detailed information on a huge range of graduate-level jobs, including entry requirements and training. Click on 'Jobs and work', then 'Explore types of jobs'.

This is the UK's official graduate careers website and has comprehensive information and advice not only on careers but also on employers, job sectors and postgraduate options.

Books in the *UCAS Progression Series* cover topics such as an introduction to the subject areas, career options, entry routes and entry requirements. Relevant titles in this series are:

Progression to Art and Design, £15.99

Progression to Media and Performing Arts, £15.99.

VT Lifeskills publish a series of careers books called the *Working in* guides, £8.50 each. These are not aimed specifically at graduates but at a wider audience. Relevant titles are:

Working in Art & Design

Working in Creative & Media

Working in Cultural Heritage

Working in English

Working in Marketing, Advertising & PR

Working in Music

Working in Politics & Law

Working in the Environment

The *Careers Uncovered* series, published by Trotman, £12.99, takes a look at a range of professional careers and gives facts, such as potential salary and working conditions, and advice on how to get into each industry. Relevant titles are:

Careers Uncovered: Journalism

Careers Uncovered: Media

Careers Uncovered: Music Industry

Careers Uncovered: Performing Arts

Inside Careers specialises in graduate careers information and jobs in the areas of business & management, city & finance and engineering & technology. Visit www.insidecareers.co.uk for detailed information on careers and opportunities in these sectors.

Graduate recruitment and postgraduate study

Graduate Prospects produces the following range of publications, which provides career and postgraduate study advice and opportunities for students and graduates. Current students can get these publications free from most university careers services and also view many products online at www.prospects.ac.uk.

Prospects Directory, a comprehensive directory of over 300 graduate recruiters with job opportunities for final-year students, published annually in September.

Prospects Finalist contains job vacancies for final-year students, published five times a year (October to May).

Prospects Graduate, a digital magazine for graduates published online every fortnight, carries graduate jobs and postgraduate courses.

Prospects Postgrad, information on postgraduate courses and research opportunities, published three times a year (in the autumn, spring and summer).

Prospects Postgraduate Directory Volume 1 Arts and Humanities, published annually in September. Details on all UK postgraduate arts and humanities courses. May be available as reference only.

Prospects Work Experience, a work-experience magazine for pre-final year students, published annually in October.

'GET', a site from Hobsons, gives you access to graduate jobs, independent careers advice and a community of job hunters at www.get.hobsons.co.uk.

'Target Jobs' is a graduate recruitment and careers advice site. You can search graduate employers, internships and jobs, as well as read information on a range of key graduate sectors at www.targetjobs.co.uk.

If you're looking for further study or work in Europe then 'Target Jobs Europe' is another useful site. You can find information on further study in Europe, as well as internships, business sectors, employer profiles and country profiles on 18 of Europe's key countries at www.targetjobseurope.com.

If you're looking more generally at working/studying abroad then the 'Prospects' website has information on working and studying in over 50 countries throughout the world. Click on 'Careers advice', then 'Country specific information' at www.prospects.ac.uk.

Index

More titles in the Student Helpbook series ...

helping students of all ages make the right choices about their careers and education.

Careers with a Science Degree – Over 100 job ideas to inspire you

An excellent read for anyone considering science at degree level.

5th edition £12.99   ISBN: 978-1-904979-39-5

Which A levels? – The guide to choosing A levels, Advanced Diplomas and other post-16 qualifications

The highly popular, student-friendly guide. Features over 50 A level subjects and the range of Advanced Diplomas. Includes career options after A levels/Advanced Diplomas and as a graduate.

7th edition £14.99   ISBN: 978-1-904979-41-8

Jobs and Careers after A levels and equivalent advanced qualifications

Opportunities for students leaving school or college at 18, including advice on job-hunting, applications and interviews.

9th edition £11.99   ISBN: 978-1-904979-21-0

CVs and Applications

For anyone who is applying for a job or college place; includes details of how to use the internet in marketing yourself.

7th edition £12.99   ISBN: 978-1-904979-44-9

Excel at Interviews

This highly successful book makes invaluable reading for students and jobhunters.

6th edition £11.99   ISBN: 978-1-904979-22-7

Visit us online to view our full range of resources at: www.lifetime-publishing.co.uk